3B

Math in Focus
Singapore Math®
by Marshall Cavendish

Workbook

Consultant and Author
Dr. Fong Ho Kheong

Authors
Chelvi Ramakrishnan and Michelle Choo

U.S. Consultants
Dr. Richard Bisk, Andy Clark, and Patsy F. Kanter

mc Marshall Cavendish
Education

U.S. Distributor

Houghton
Mifflin
Harcourt

© 2015 Marshall Cavendish Education Pte Ltd

Published by Marshall Cavendish Education
An imprint of Marshall Cavendish Education Pte Ltd
Times Centre, 1 New Industrial Road, Singapore 536196
Customer Service Hotline: (65) 6213 9444
US Office Tel: (1-914) 332 8888 Fax: (1-914) 332 8882
E-mail: tmesales@mceducation.com
Website: www.mceducation.com

Distributed by
Houghton Mifflin Harcourt
222 Berkeley Street
Boston, MA 02116
Tel: 617-351-5000
Website: www.hmheducation.com/mathinfocus

First published 2015

Math in Focus® Workbook 3B
ISBN 978-0-544-19385-7

Printed in Singapore

4 5 6 7 8   1401   20 19 18 17 16 15
4500543034   A B C D E

Contents

10 Money

11 Metric Length, Mass, and Volume

12 Real-World Problems: Measurement

13 Bar Graphs and Line Plots

14 Fractions

Customary Length, Weight, and Capacity

Time and Temperature

17 Angles and Lines

18 Two-Dimensional Shapes

19 Area and Perimeter

Name: _____ **Date:** _____

Money

Practice 1 Addition

Add mentally.

1. $7.30 + $2.00 = $_____   **2.** $37.20 + $0.45 = $_____

3. $5.20 + $12.65 = $_____   **4.** $51.20 + $14.80 = $_____

5. $0.95 + $9.35 = $_____   **6.** $4.35 + $64.85 = $_____

7. $31.65 + $3.90 = $_____   **8.** $5.45 + $0.75 = $_____

Find each missing amount.

9. $26.40 + $72.50 = $_____

$26 40¢ $72 50¢

$26 + $72 = $_____

40¢ + 50¢ = _____¢

$_____ + _____¢ = $_____

10. $51.25 + $4.20 = $_____

$51 25¢ $4 20¢

$_____ + $_____ = $_____

_____¢ + _____¢ = _____¢

$_____ + _____¢ = $_____

Find each missing amount.

11. $6.05 + $18.20 = $_____

$6 5¢ $18 20¢

$_____ + $_____ = $_____

_____¢ + _____¢ = _____¢

$_____ + _____¢ = $_____

12. $60.05 + $17.70 = $_____

$60 5¢ $17 70¢

$_____ + $_____ = $_____

_____¢ + _____¢ = _____¢

$_____ + _____¢ = $_____

Use the items and prices in the picture to answer each exercise.

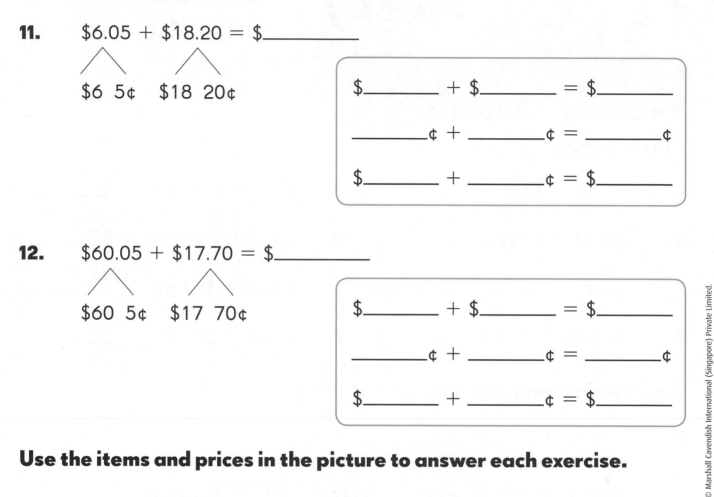

oranges $9.45   cheese $3.55   milk $2.70   broccoli $2.30

biscuits $3.05   grapes $12.95   cucumber $0.85   cabbage $1.15

What is the cost of

13. a carton of milk and a head of broccoli? $_____

14. a bunch of grapes and a packet of wholemeal biscuits? $_____

15. a cucumber and a head of cabbage? $_____

16. a pack of cheese and a box of oranges? $_____

Practice 2   Addition

Complete each number bond. Then add.

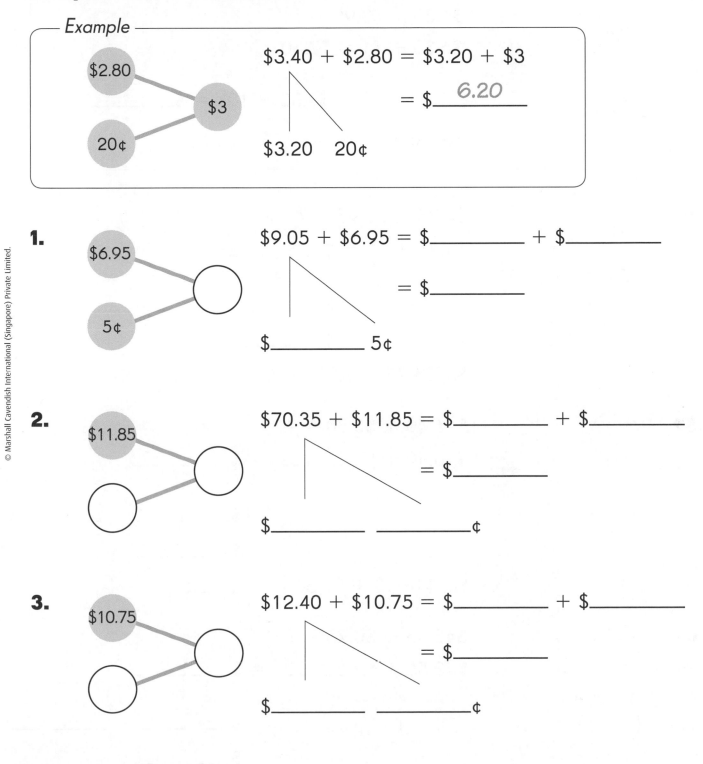

Example

$2.80 20¢ $3

$3.40 + $2.80 = $3.20 + $3

$3.20   20¢

= $ _6.20_

1.

$6.95   5¢

$9.05 + $6.95 = $ _____ + $ _____

= $ _____

$ _____ 5¢

2.

$11.85

$70.35 + $11.85 = $ _____ + $ _____

= $ _____

$ _____ _____ ¢

3.

$10.75

$12.40 + $10.75 = $ _____ + $ _____

= $ _____

$ _____ _____ ¢

Complete each number bond. Then add.

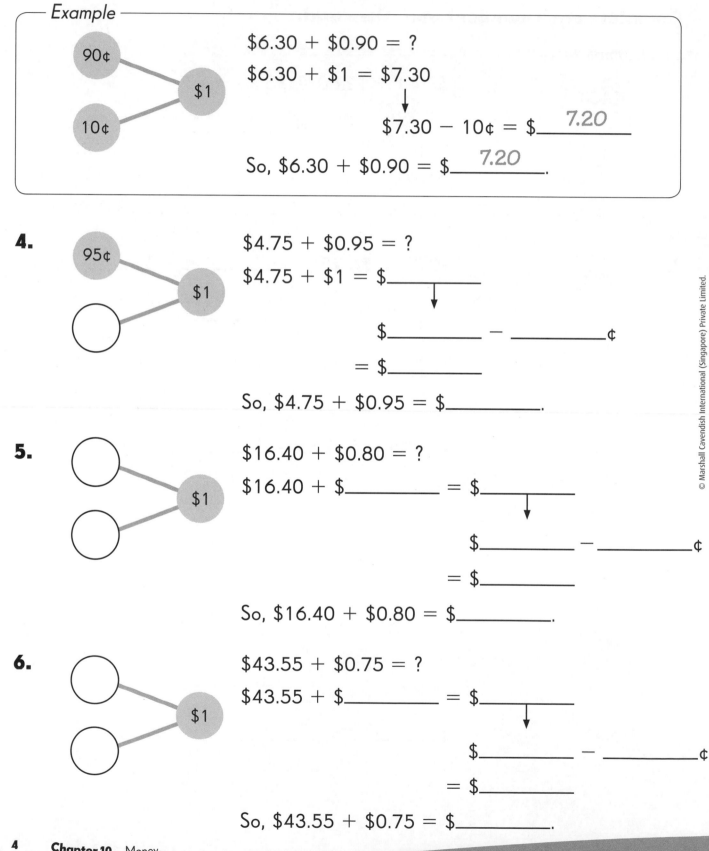

Example

90¢, 10¢, $1

$6.30 + $0.90 = ?

$6.30 + $1 = $7.30

$7.30 − 10¢ = $___7.20___

So, $6.30 + $0.90 = $___7.20___.

4.

95¢, ◯, $1

$4.75 + $0.95 = ?

$4.75 + $1 = $_____

$_____ − _____¢

= $_____

So, $4.75 + $0.95 = $_____.

5.

◯, ◯, $1

$16.40 + $0.80 = ?

$16.40 + $_____ = $_____

$_____ − _____¢

= $_____

So, $16.40 + $0.80 = $_____.

6.

◯, ◯, $1

$43.55 + $0.75 = ?

$43.55 + $_____ = $_____

$_____ − _____¢

= $_____

So, $43.55 + $0.75 = $_____.

Practice 3   Addition

Change dollars and cents to cents. Then add.

Add as you would whole numbers.

┌─ *Example* ─────────────────────────────────┐

$2.30   2 3 0
+ $6.20   + 6 2 0
─────────   ─────────
$8.50   850

└──┘

1. $14.70
+ $20.15
─────────
(A) $

2. $65.05
+ $ 0.95
─────────
(M) $

3. $20.70
+ $35.55
─────────
(T) $

4. $ 3.65
+ $32.75
─────────
(R) $

5. $ 4.65
+ $73.25
─────────
(S) $

6. $93.20
+ $ 5.95
─────────
(C) $

7. $15.85
+ $24.15
─────────
(I) $

8. $25.25
+ $28.75
─────────
(G) $

Write the letter that matches each answer to find out.

9.   How do you thank a person in Spanish?

_____ _____ _____ _____ _____ _____ _____
$54.00 $36.40 $34.85 $99.15 $40.00 $34.85 $77.90

Look at the picture. Write the prices, and then add.

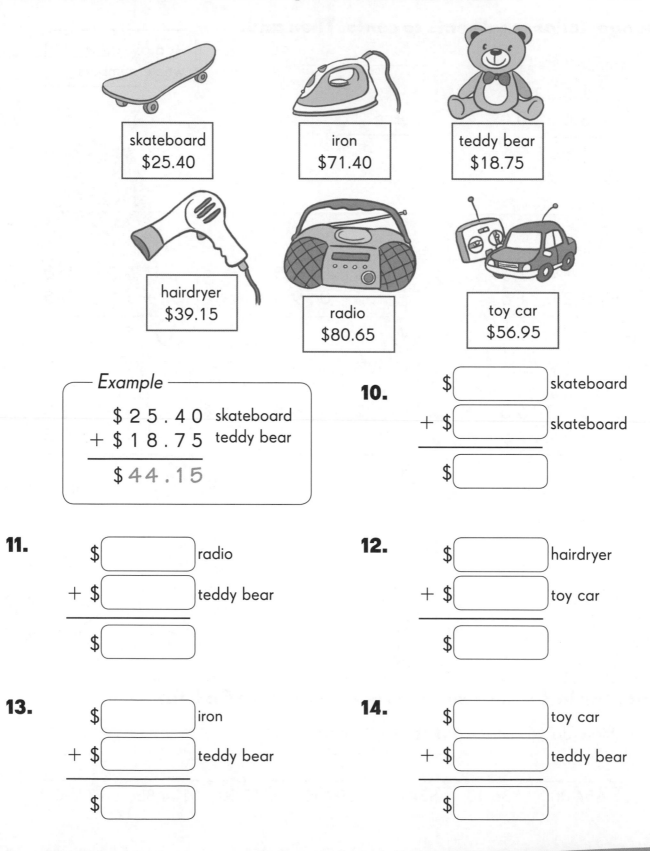

skateboard
$25.40

iron
$71.40

teddy bear
$18.75

hairdryer
$39.15

radio
$80.65

toy car
$56.95

Example

$ 2 5 . 4 0   skateboard
+ $ 1 8 . 7 5   teddy bear
$ 4 4 . 1 5

10. $ ☐   skateboard
+ $ ☐   skateboard
$ ☐

11. $ ☐   radio
+ $ ☐   teddy bear
$ ☐

12. $ ☐   hairdryer
+ $ ☐   toy car
$ ☐

13. $ ☐   iron
+ $ ☐   teddy bear
$ ☐

14. $ ☐   toy car
+ $ ☐   teddy bear
$ ☐

Practice 4 Subtraction

Subtract. Color the answers on the picture.

1. $6.35 − $6.00 = $_____   **2.** $8.35 − $5.00   = $_____

3. $98.20 − $8.00 = $_____   **4.** $76.65 − $12.00 = $_____

5. $26.40 − $9.00 = $_____   **6.** $45.60 − $39.00 = $_____

7. $5.25 − $0.05 = $_____   **8.** $1.45 − $0.35   = $_____

9. $14.90 − $0.70 = $_____   **10.** $20.75 − $0.30 = $_____

11. $15.60 − $0.35 = $_____   **12.** $26.70 − $0.45 = $_____

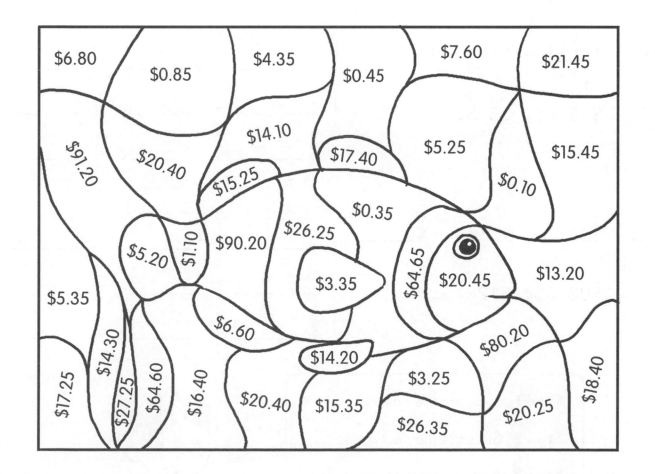

Subtract.

13. $3.20 − $1.15 = $_____

$3   20¢ $1   15¢

$3 − $1 = $_____

20¢ − 15¢ = _____¢

$_____ + _____¢ = $_____

14. $10.50 − $2.50 = $_____

$10   50¢ $2   50¢

$_____ − $_____ = $_____

_____¢ − _____¢ = _____¢

$_____ + _____¢ = $_____

15. $65.65 − $3.05 = $_____

$65   65¢ $3   5¢

$_____ − $_____ = $_____

_____¢ − _____¢ = _____¢

$_____ + _____¢ = $_____

16. $83.55 − $12.45 = $_____

$83   55¢ $12   45¢

$_____ − $_____ = $_____

_____¢ − _____¢ = _____¢

$_____ + _____¢ = $_____

Step 1 Subtract the dollars.

Step 2 Subtract the cents.

Step 3 Add the cents to the dollars.

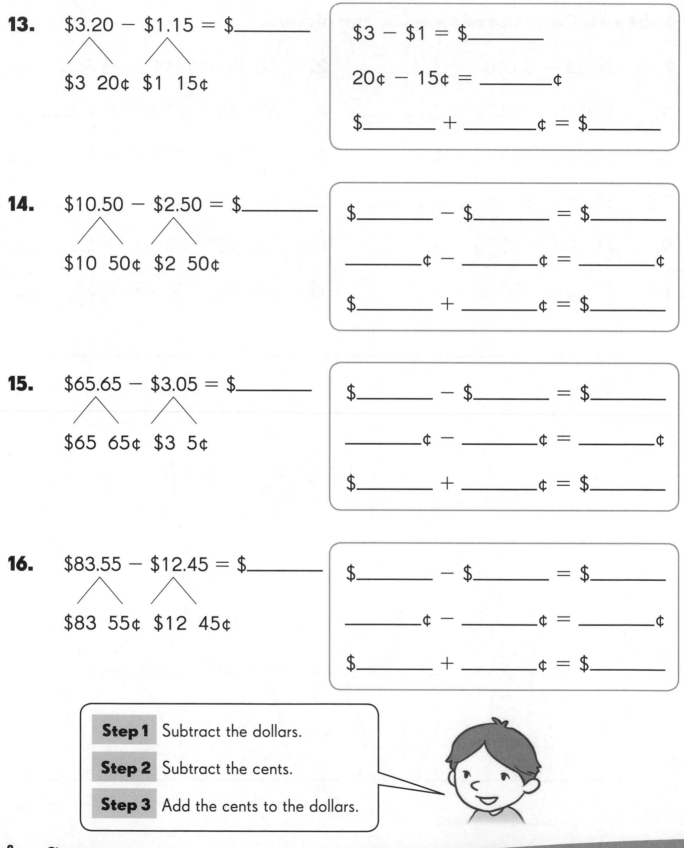

Practice 5 Subtraction

Complete each number bond. Then subtract.

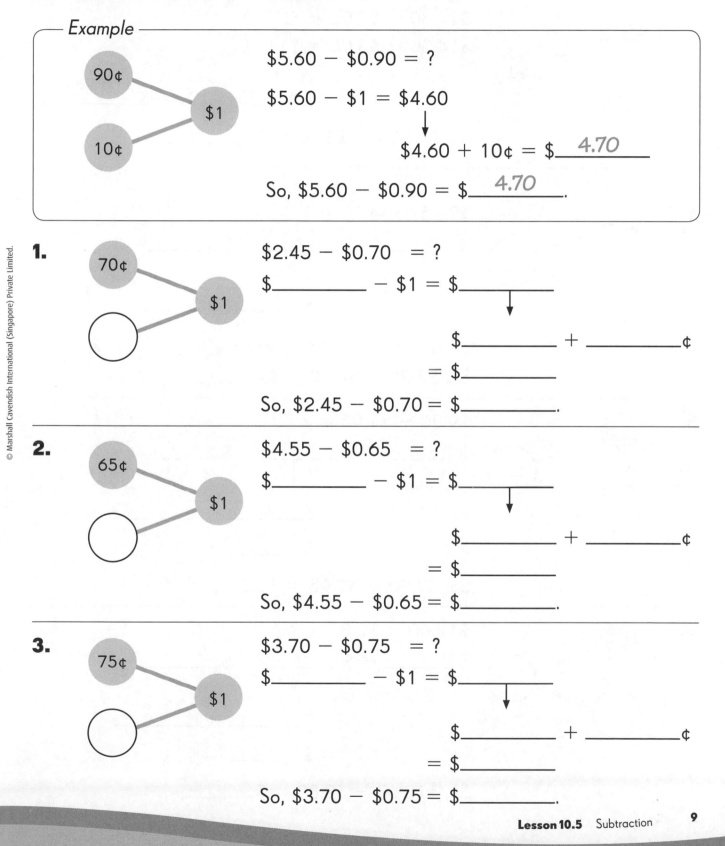

Example

90¢ \
      $1 \
10¢

$5.60 − $0.90 = ?

$5.60 − $1 = $4.60

         ↓

      $4.60 + 10¢ = $___4.70___

So, $5.60 − $0.90 = $___4.70___.

1.

70¢ \
      $1 \
◯

$2.45 − $0.70 = ?

$_____ − $1 = $_____

         ↓

$_____ + _____¢

= $_____

So, $2.45 − $0.70 = $_____.

2.

65¢ \
      $1 \
◯

$4.55 − $0.65 = ?

$_____ − $1 = $_____

         ↓

$_____ + _____¢

= $_____

So, $4.55 − $0.65 = $_____.

3.

75¢ \
      $1 \
◯

$3.70 − $0.75 = ?

$_____ − $1 = $_____

         ↓

$_____ + _____¢

= $_____

So, $3.70 − $0.75 = $_____.

Complete each number bond. Then subtract.

Example

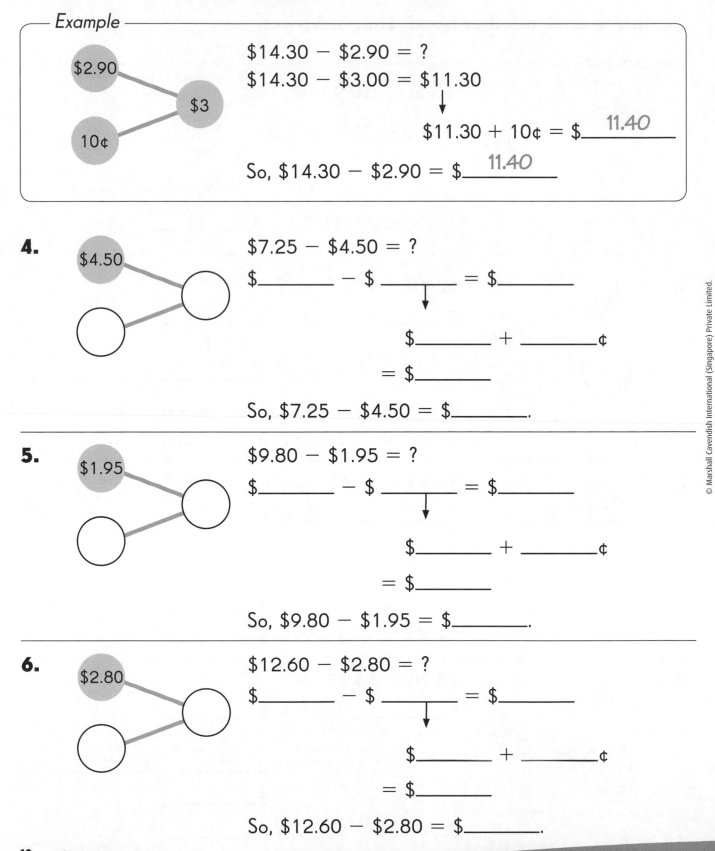

$2.90
$3
10¢

$14.30 − $2.90 = ?
$14.30 − $3.00 = $11.30

$11.30 + 10¢ = $__11.40__

So, $14.30 − $2.90 = $__11.40__

4.

$4.50

$7.25 − $4.50 = ?

$_____ − $ _____ = $_____

$_____ + _____¢

= $_____

So, $7.25 − $4.50 = $_____.

5.

$1.95

$9.80 − $1.95 = ?

$_____ − $ _____ = $_____

$_____ + _____¢

= $_____

So, $9.80 − $1.95 = $_____.

6.

$2.80

$12.60 − $2.80 = ?

$_____ − $ _____ = $_____

$_____ + _____¢

= $_____

So, $12.60 − $2.80 = $_____.

Practice 6 Subtraction

Change dollars and cents to cents. Then subtract.

Example

$12.35	1235
− $ 4.25	− 425
$ 8.10	810

Subtract as you would whole numbers.

1. $17.55
     − $ 3.20
  (a) $

2. $4.25
     − $3.65
  (s) $

3. $5.00
     − $0.75
  (c) $

4. $10.15
     − $ 7.30
  (r) $

5. $76.55
     − $47.85
  (e) $

6. $55.80
     − $10.95
  (l) $

7. $79.40
     − $33.45
  (g) $

8. $40.00
     − $15.85
  (n) $

Write the letter that matches each answer to complete the sentence.

9.   Let's keep our national parks

_____ _____ _____ _____ _____ and
$4.25 $44.85 $28.70 $14.35 $24.15

_____ _____ _____ _____ _____ .
$45.95 $2.85 $28.70 $28.70 $24.15

Find the amount of change you will receive.

	Amount I Have	Title and Cost of Book	Subtraction	Change
10.		 Snow White $3.85	$ 4.00 − $ 3.85 ———— $ 0.15	$0.15
11.		 Encyclopedia $85		
12.		 Hansel and Gretel $8.65		
13.		 THE ANIMAL BOOK $12.30		

Practice 7 Real-World Problems: Money

Solve. Use bar models to help you.

1. Nick has $18.20.
He buys a pencil case for $12.50.
How much does he have left?

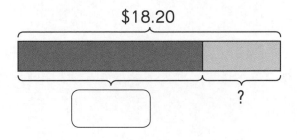

$18.20 − $12.50 = $_____

He has $_____ left.

2. Tim has $40. Tim's sister has $17.25 more.
How much does his sister have?

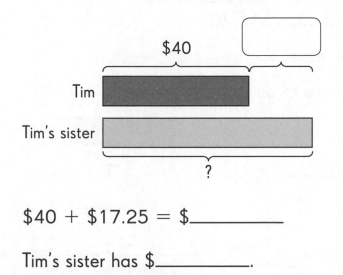

$40 + $17.25 = $_____

Tim's sister has $_____.

3. Pamela buys a dress for $35.70. She buys a pair of shoes that costs $3.20 more than the dress.

   a. How much is the pair of shoes?

   b. How much does she spend in all?

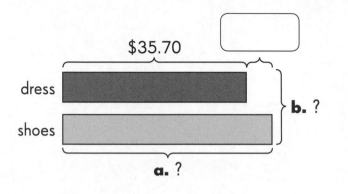

   a. $35.70 + $3.20 = $_____

      The pair of shoes is $_____.

   b. $35.70 + $_____ = $_____

      She spends $_____ in all.

4. Roberto has $7.85 to start with. Then he saves $2.40. He wants to buy a football that costs $16.70.

   a. How much money does he have?

   b. How much more must he save to buy the football?

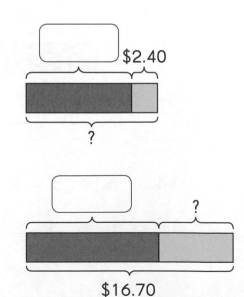

   a. $7.85 + $2.40 = $_____

      He has $_____.

   b. $16.70 − $_____ = $_____

      He must save $_____ more.

Practice 8 Real-World Problems: Money

Solve.
Draw bar models to help you.

1. Mrs. Twohill buys a bottle of cooking oil for $6.75.
She gives the cashier two $5 bills.
How much change does she receive?

2. Mr. Larson spends $37.50 at a supermarket.
He spends $8.25 less than Mrs. Rosa.
How much does Mrs. Rosa spend?

Solve. Draw bar models to help you.

3.   Lisa buys a tennis racket and a can of tennis balls.
The can of tennis balls costs $18.60. The racket costs $40.85 more.

    a.   How much is the racket?

    b.   How much does she spend in all?

4.   Jacob has $8.65 to take to the fair. His mother gives him $15.50 more.
He spends $16.45 at the fair.

    a.   How much does he bring to the fair?

    b.   How much does he have left?

5. Madi buys a carton of milk and a bag of bagels.
She gives the cashier $10 and receives $5.25 change.
The bag of bagels costs $2.75.
How much does the carton of milk cost?

First, find out how much the milk and bagels cost.

6. Jordan saved $10.40 last month.
He saved $5.50 less this month.
How much did he save in the two months?

7. A board game costs $28.45.
It is $15.20 more than a paint set.
The paint set costs $7.90 more than a toy car.
How much does the toy car cost?

8. Tim and Karen each had the same amount of money to start with.
Karen pays $24.60 for a CD and has $7.50 left.
Tim buys a watch for $22.75.
How much money does Tim have left?

Math Journal

Solve. Use bar models to help you.
Choose whether to add or subtract. Then solve.

1. Lynn spends $5.20 on breakfast. She spends $1.85 more on breakfast than on dinner. How much does she spend on both meals?

Step 1

Draw the bar model.

$5.20

breakfast

dinner

?

? $1.85

Step 2

Find _____.

Add / Subtract $_____ from $_____.

$_____ ◯ $_____ = $_____

Step 3

Find _____.

Add / Subtract $_____ to $_____.

$_____ ◯ $_____ = $_____

She spends $_____ on both meals.

Look at the problem. Then find the mistake.

Aaron made a mistake while subtracting.

$$\begin{array}{r} \$15.25 \\ - \$\ 8.40 \\ \hline \$\ 7.85 \end{array}$$

2.   Was the mistake made in subtracting the cents? _____

3.   Was the mistake made in subtracting the dollars? _____

4.   Find the correct answer.

$$\begin{array}{r} \$15.25 \\ - \$\ 8.40 \\ \hline \$ \end{array}$$

Here's another problem with a mistake.

$$\begin{array}{r} \$\ 9.95 \\ + \$\ 7.30 \\ \hline \$16.25 \end{array}$$

5.   What is the mistake?

_____

6.   Find the correct answer.

$$\begin{array}{r} \$\ 9.95 \\ + \$\ 7.30 \\ \hline \$ \end{array}$$

Put On Your Thinking Cap!

Challenging Practice

Look at the pictures. Solve the real-world problems.

1.   Ms. O'Brien needs to get 6 bottles of shampoo
     for her childcare center. How much will she spend?

$5.50 each

Buy 2 get 1 free

2.   Mrs. Keith wants to spend the least amount of money to buy 3 gallons of
     milk. Which bottle should she buy?

$1.85 $3.79

$\frac{1}{2}$-gallon   1-gallon

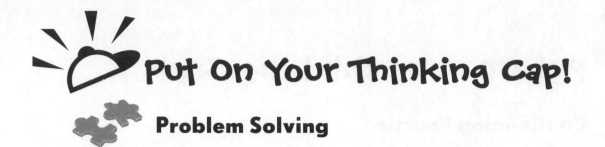

Put On Your Thinking Cap!

Problem Solving

Solve.

1. Harry has some money. His sister has $75.10. After he gives $28 to his mother, he has $15.20 less than his sister. How much does Harry have at first?

2. Kate saves some money. She saves only dimes and quarters. She has the same number of dimes and quarters. There are less than 12 coins but more than 5 coins altogether. How much could she have saved?

There is more than 1 answer.

Chapter 11 Metric Length, Mass, and Volume

Practice 1 Meters and Centimeters

Complete.

┌─ *Example* ─────────────────────────────────────┐

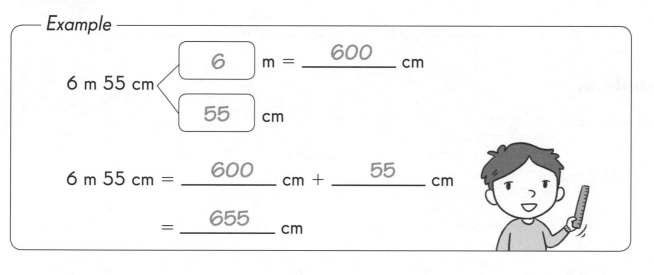

6 m 55 cm ⟨ 6 ⟩ m = ___600___ cm

55 cm

6 m 55 cm = ___600___ cm + ___55___ cm

= ___655___ cm

└──┘

1.

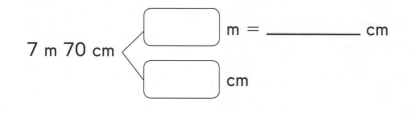

7 m 70 cm ⟨ ▭ ⟩ m = _____ cm

▭ cm

7 m 70 cm = _____ cm + _____ cm

= _____ cm

2.

8 m 1 cm ⟨ ▭ ⟩ m = _____ cm

▭ cm

8 m 1 cm = _____ cm + _____ cm

= _____ cm

Write in centimeters.

3. 6 m 96 cm = _____ cm + _____ cm = _____ cm

4. 8 m 90 cm = _____ cm + _____ cm = _____ cm

5. 9 m 20 cm = _____ cm + _____ cm = _____ cm

6. 9 m 2 cm = _____ cm + _____ cm = _____ cm

Complete.

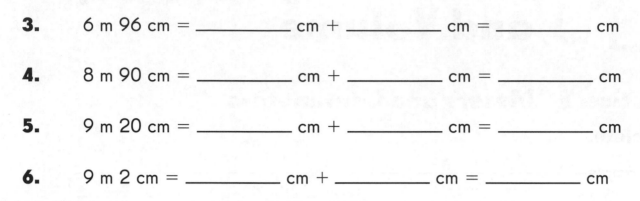

Example

212 cm
- 200 cm = __2__ m
- 12 cm

212 cm = __2__ m __12__ cm

7.

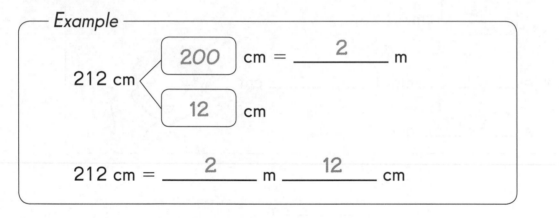

428 cm
- _____ cm = _____ m
- _____ cm

428 cm = _____ m _____ cm

8.

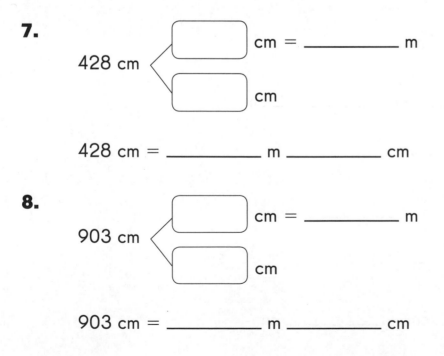

903 cm
- _____ cm = _____ m
- _____ cm

903 cm = _____ m _____ cm

Write in meters and centimeters.

9. 123 cm = _____ cm + _____ cm = _____ m _____ cm

10. 390 cm = _____ cm + _____ cm = _____ m _____ cm

11. 365 cm = _____ cm + _____ cm = _____ m _____ cm

12. 909 cm = _____ cm + _____ cm = _____ m _____ cm

Choose the unit you would use to measure each.
Write *meters* or *centimeters*.

13.

This pine tree is about 2 _____ tall.

14.

The insect is about 10 _____ long.

Fill in the blanks.

Color the banner with the longest measurement.

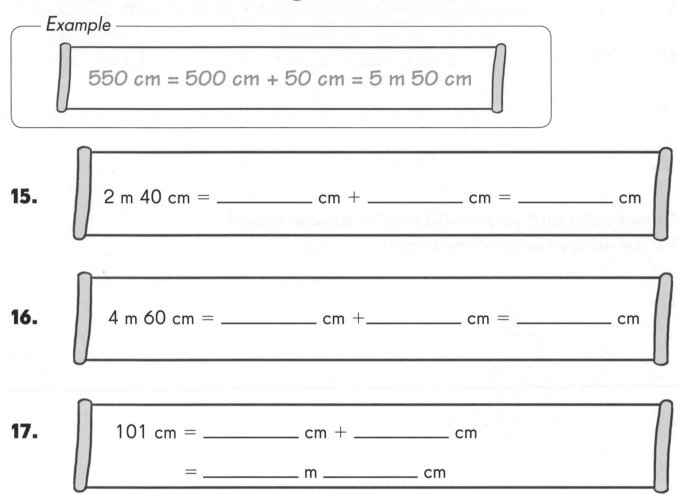

Example

550 cm = 500 cm + 50 cm = 5 m 50 cm

15. 2 m 40 cm = _____ cm + _____ cm = _____ cm

16. 4 m 60 cm = _____ cm + _____ cm = _____ cm

17. 101 cm = _____ cm + _____ cm

= _____ m _____ cm

Color the boxes with equal measurements.

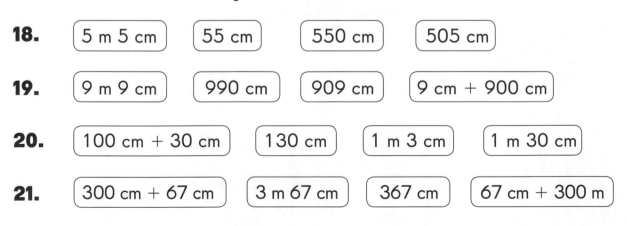

18. | 5 m 5 cm | 55 cm | 550 cm | 505 cm |

19. | 9 m 9 cm | 990 cm | 909 cm | 9 cm + 900 cm |

20. | 100 cm + 30 cm | 130 cm | 1 m 3 cm | 1 m 30 cm |

21. | 300 cm + 67 cm | 3 m 67 cm | 367 cm | 67 cm + 300 m |

Practice 2 Kilometers and Meters

Complete.

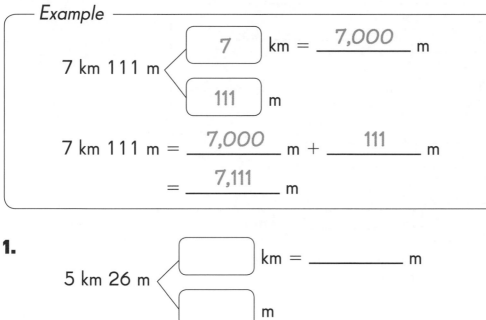

Example

7 km 111 m

| 7 | km = __7,000__ m |
| 111 | m |

7 km 111 m = __7,000__ m + __111__ m

= __7,111__ m

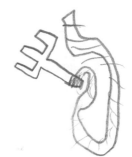

1.

5 km 26 m

| | km = _____ m |
| | m |

5 km 26 m = _____ m + _____ m

= _____ m

2.

8 km 8 m

| | km = _____ m |
| | m |

8 km 8 m = _____ m + _____ m

= _____ m

Write in meters.

3. 5 km 505 m = _____ m + _____ m = _____ m

4. 8 km 500 m = _____ m + _____ m = _____ m

5. 8 km 50 m = _____ m + _____ m = _____ m

6. 9 km 5 m = _____ m + _____ m = _____ m

Complete.

Example

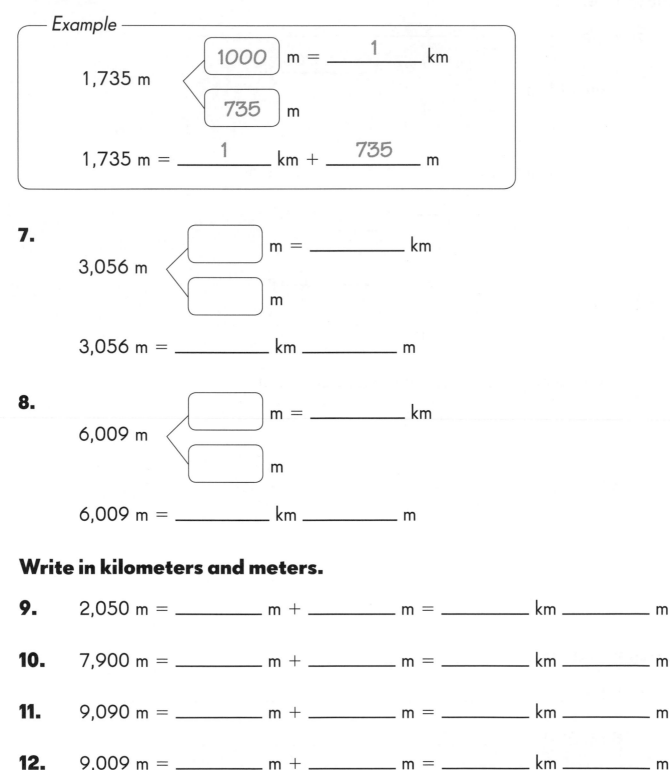

1,735 m

1000 m = ____1____ km

735 m

1,735 m = ____1____ km + ____735____ m

7.

3,056 m

_____ m = _____ km

_____ m

3,056 m = _____ km _____ m

8.

6,009 m

_____ m = _____ km

_____ m

6,009 m = _____ km _____ m

Write in kilometers and meters.

9. 2,050 m = _____ m + _____ m = _____ km _____ m

10. 7,900 m = _____ m + _____ m = _____ km _____ m

11. 9,090 m = _____ m + _____ m = _____ km _____ m

12. 9,009 m = _____ m + _____ m = _____ km _____ m

Choose the unit you would use to measure each.
Write *kilometers* or *meters*.

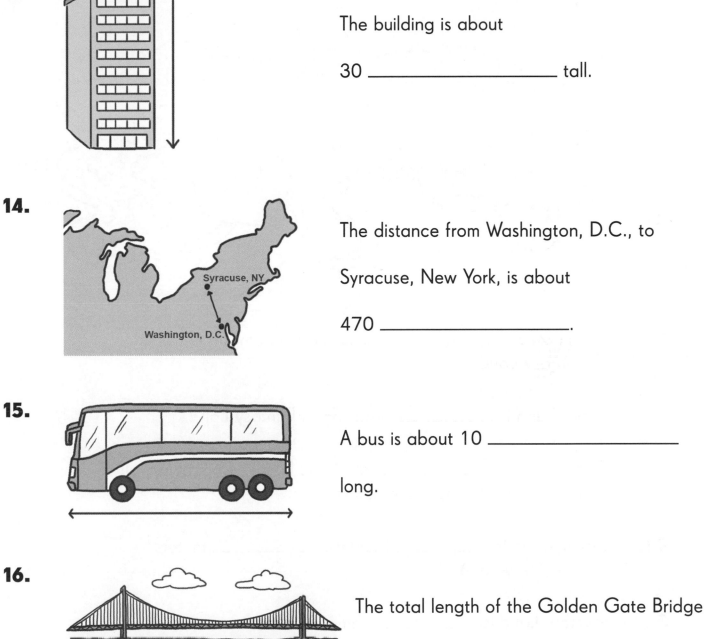

13.

The building is about

30 _____ tall.

14.

The distance from Washington, D.C., to

Syracuse, New York, is about

470 _____.

15.

A bus is about 10 _____

long.

16.

The total length of the Golden Gate Bridge

is about 3 _____.

Complete.

Jacob is at an amusement park. He wants to visit all four theme parks.
Find the length of each path he wants to take.

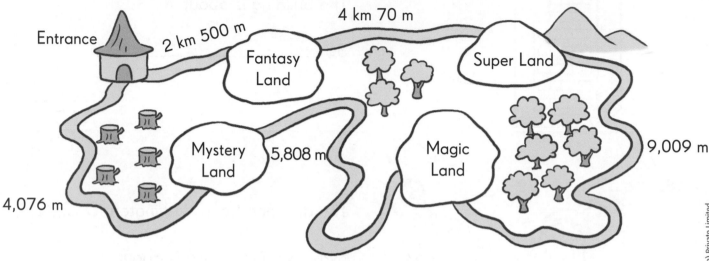

17. Jacob needs to travel _____ meters from the entrance to Fantasy Land.

18. Super Land is _____ meters from Fantasy Land.

19. From _____ to Magic Land, he has to travel a distance of 9 kilometers 9 meters.

20. Magic Land is _____ kilometers _____ meters from Mystery Land.

21. Mystery Land is _____ kilometers _____ meters from the entrance.

Practice 3   Kilograms and Grams

Read the scales. Write the mass.

1.

_____ kg

2.

_____ g

3.

_____ kg _____ g

4.

_____ kg _____ g

5.

_____ g

6.

_____ kg _____ g

Complete.

7.

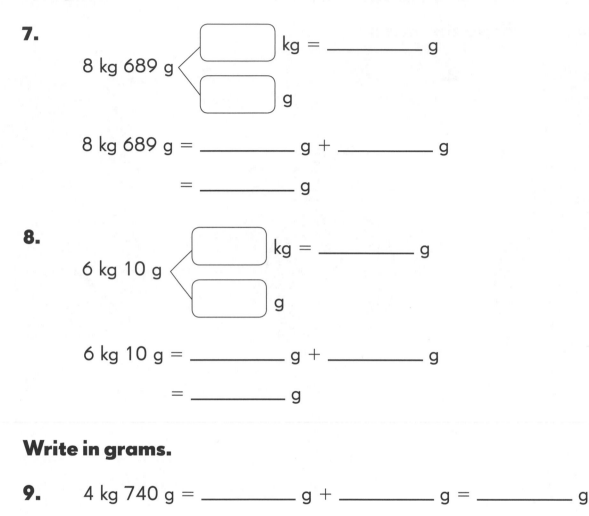

8 kg 689 g
```
┌──────────┐
│          │ kg = _____ g
└──────────┘
┌──────────┐
│          │ g
└──────────┘
```

8 kg 689 g = _____ g + _____ g

= _____ g

8.

6 kg 10 g
```
┌──────────┐
│          │ kg = _____ g
└──────────┘
┌──────────┐
│          │ g
└──────────┘
```

6 kg 10 g = _____ g + _____ g

= _____ g

Write in grams.

9.   4 kg 740 g = _____ g + _____ g = _____ g

10. 5 kg 123 g = _____ g + _____ g = _____ g

11. 3 kg 40 g = _____ g + _____ g = _____ g

12. 6 kg 8 g = _____ g + _____ g = _____ g

Complete.

13.

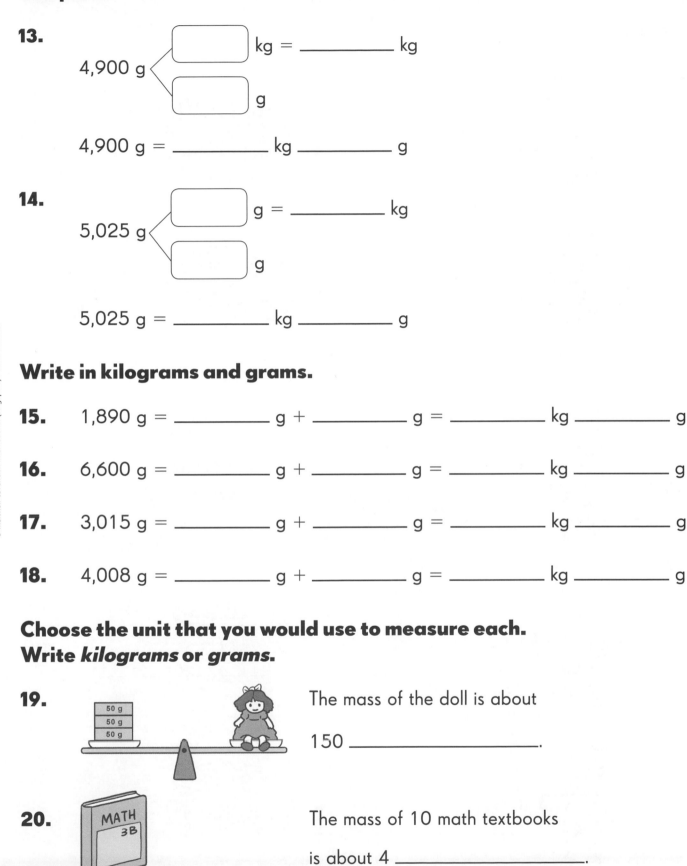

4,900 g [☐ kg = _____ kg]
         [☐ g]

4,900 g = _____ kg _____ g

14.

5,025 g [☐ g = _____ kg]
         [☐ g]

5,025 g = _____ kg _____ g

Write in kilograms and grams.

15. 1,890 g = _____ g + _____ g = _____ kg _____ g

16. 6,600 g = _____ g + _____ g = _____ kg _____ g

17. 3,015 g = _____ g + _____ g = _____ kg _____ g

18. 4,008 g = _____ g + _____ g = _____ kg _____ g

Choose the unit that you would use to measure each.
Write *kilograms* or *grams*.

19.

The mass of the doll is about

150 _____.

20.

MATH
3B

The mass of 10 math textbooks

is about 4 _____.

Match.

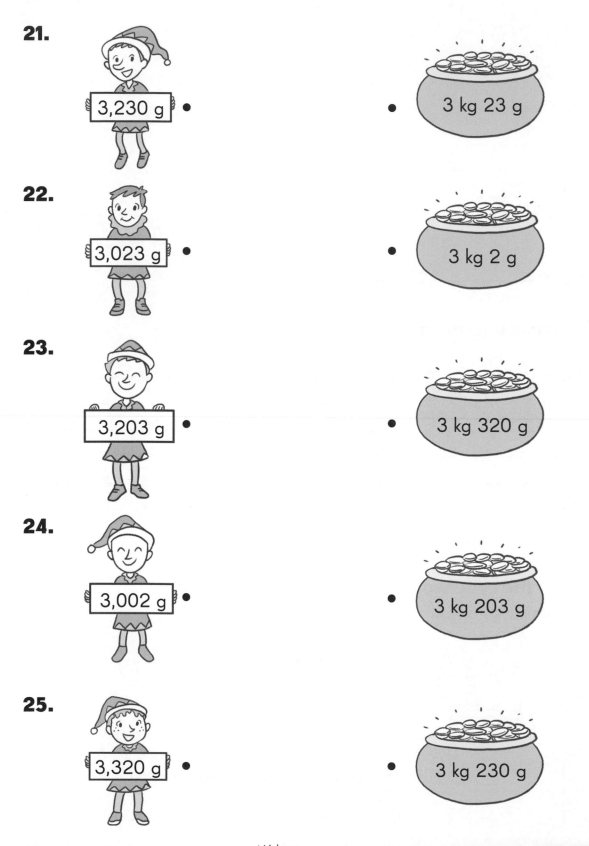

21. 3,230 g •   • 3 kg 23 g

22. 3,023 g •   • 3 kg 2 g

23. 3,203 g •   • 3 kg 320 g

24. 3,002 g •   • 3 kg 203 g

25. 3,320 g •   • 3 kg 230 g

Practice 4   Liters and Milliliters

Find the volume of water in each measuring cup.

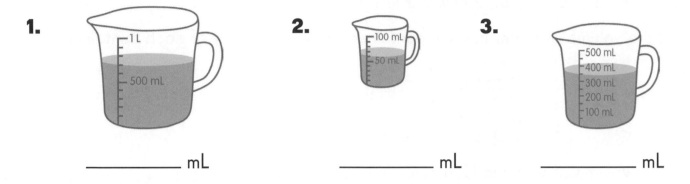

1. _____ mL

2. _____ mL

3. _____ mL

The water from each container is poured into measuring cups. Find the capacity of each container.

4.

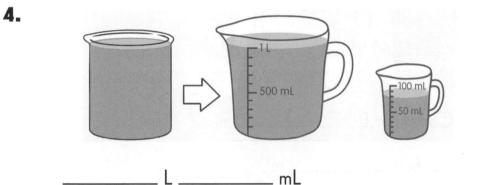

_____ L _____ mL

5.

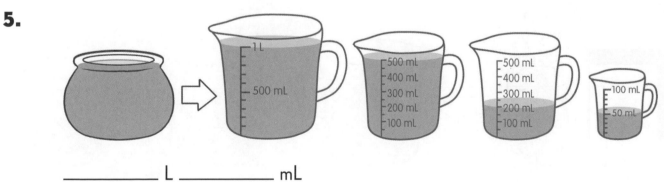

_____ L _____ mL

Complete.

A teacher filled Containers A and B completely with water.

However, he had only enough water left to fill $\frac{1}{2}$ of Container C.

Find the volume of water in each container and the capacity of each container.

6.

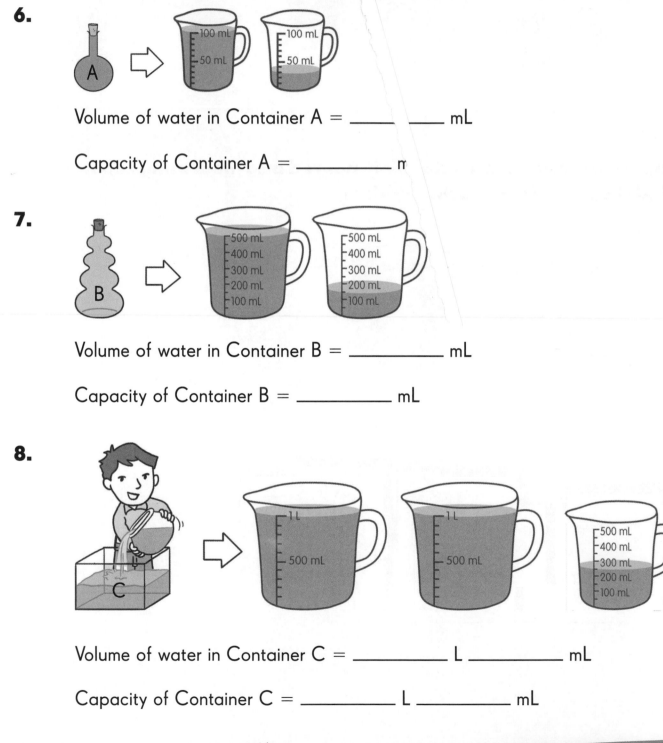

Volume of water in Container A = _____ _____ mL

Capacity of Container A = _____ m

7.

Volume of water in Container B = _____ mL

Capacity of Container B = _____ mL

8.

Volume of water in Container C = _____ L _____ mL

Capacity of Container C = _____ L _____ mL

Complete.

9.

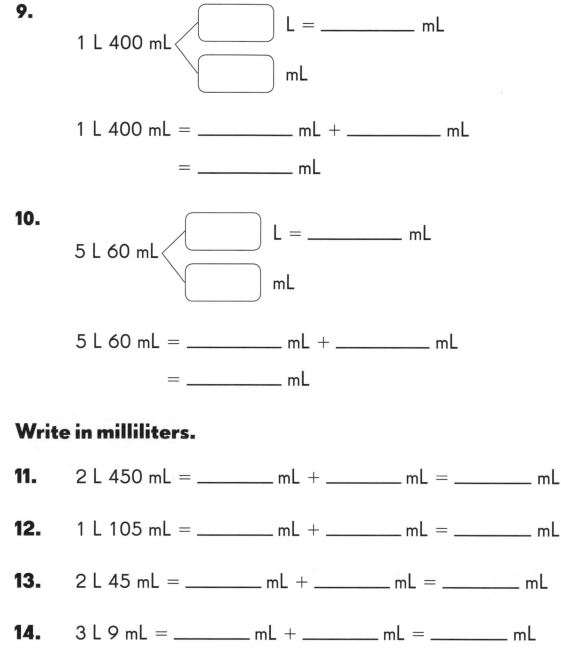

1 L 400 mL ⟨ ▢ L = _____ mL

▢ mL

1 L 400 mL = _____ mL + _____ mL

= _____ mL

10.

5 L 60 mL ⟨ ▢ L = _____ mL

▢ mL

5 L 60 mL = _____ mL + _____ mL

= _____ mL

Write in milliliters.

11.   2 L 450 mL = _____ mL + _____ mL = _____ mL

12.   1 L 105 mL = _____ mL + _____ mL = _____ mL

13.   2 L 45 mL = _____ mL + _____ mL = _____ mL

14.   3 L 9 mL = _____ mL + _____ mL = _____ mL

Complete.

15.

7,080 mL ⟨
[   ] mL = _____ L

[   ] mL

7,080 mL = _____ L _____ mL

16.

9,909 mL ⟨
[   ] mL = _____ L

[   ] mL

9,909 mL = _____ L _____ mL

Write in liters and milliliters.

17. 4,900 mL = _____ mL + _____ mL = _____ L _____ mL

18. 6,505 mL = _____ mL + _____ mL = _____ L _____ mL

19. 2,090 mL = _____ mL + _____ mL = _____ L _____ mL

20. 2,005 mL = _____ mL + _____ mL = _____ L _____ mL

Choose the unit you would use to measure each.
Write *liters* or *milliliters*.

21. 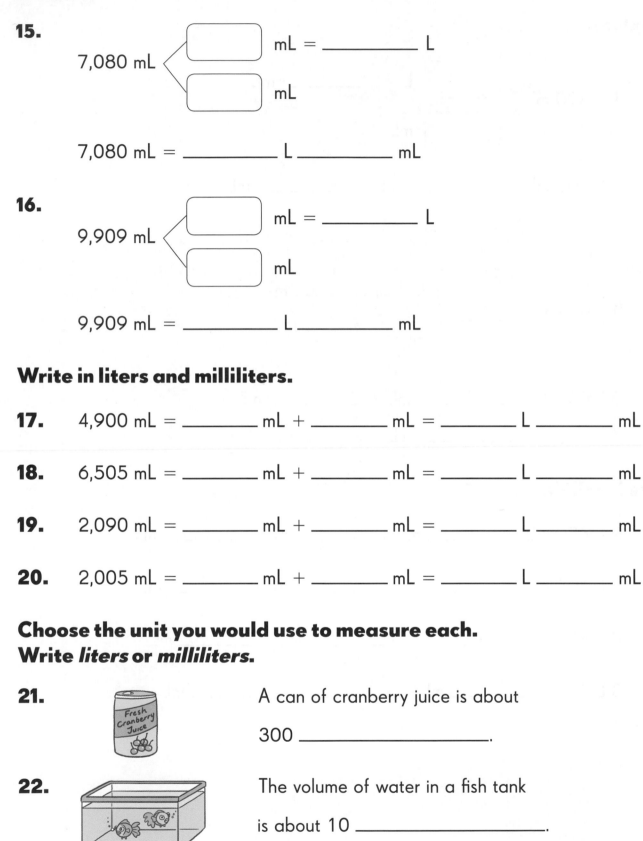 A can of cranberry juice is about

300 _____.

22. The volume of water in a fish tank

is about 10 _____.

Put On Your Thinking Cap!

Challenging Practice

Fill in the correct units of measurement.

| centimeters | kilometers | kilometer | meters |

1.   William and Burt had a race on the running track.

William took ten minutes to run one _____, while Burt took

4 minutes to run seven hundred _____.

Circle the better measurement.

2.   The height of a five-story building is 30 (meters / centimeters).

3.   The length of a desk is 1 (meter / kilometer).

4.   The weight of a large log from a tree is 18 (kilograms / grams).

5.   The weight of a pen is 10 (grams / kilograms).

6.   The capacity of a barrel is about 100 (liters / milliliters) of water.

Put On Your Thinking Cap!

Problem Solving

Find the mass of each item.

turkey   ham

turkey   lamb leg

lamb leg

7. The mass of the lamb leg is _____ kilograms.

8. The mass of the turkey is _____ kilograms.

9. The mass of the ham is _____ kilograms.

Chapter 12 Real-World Problems: Measurement

Practice 1   Real-World Problems: One-Step Problems

Solve. Use bar models to help you.

1. A restaurant has two tables of different lengths.
One is 146 centimeters long. The other is 185 centimeters long.
What is their total length?
Write your answer in meters and centimeters.

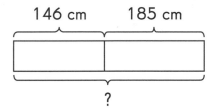

2. Jim is preparing for a race.
He runs around the track 3 times each day.
If he runs 300 meters a day, what is the length of the track?

3. A baby elephant has a mass of 145 kilograms.
The mass of its sister is 5 times as much.
What is the mass of its sister?

4. James has a fish tank with a capacity of 24 liters.
He uses a 2-liter pail to fill the tank.
How many pails of water does he use?

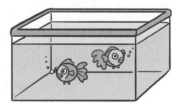

5.   A watering can contains 980 milliliters of water.
Some water is used to water the plants.
In the end, 350 milliliters of water are left.
How much water is used to water the plants?

6.   A baker has 2,000 grams of flour.
He uses 425 grams of it.
What is the mass of the flour left?
Give your answer in kilograms and grams.

7. Max buys 875 grams of nuts on Monday.
He buys 955 grams of nuts on Tuesday.
What is the total mass of nuts he buys?
Give your answer in kilograms and grams.

8. Mrs. Spence has 4 bottles of orange juice.
Each bottle contains 125 milliliters of juice.
She pours all the juice into an empty container.
How much orange juice is in the container?

Practice 2 Real-World Problems: Two-Step Problems

Solve. Draw bar models to help you.

1. The mass of a grapefruit is 1,200 grams.
    A watermelon is 850 grams heavier than the grapefruit.

    a. What is the mass of the watermelon?
    b. What is the total mass of the two fruits?

    Give your answer in kilograms and grams.

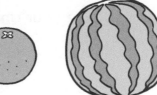

2. Box A has a mass of 35 kilograms.
    Box B is twice as heavy as Box A.
    Box C is 12 kilograms lighter than Box B.

    a. What is the mass of Box B?
    b. What is the mass of Box C?

3. Jill has 3,110 milliliters of water left after filling 3 mugs.
Each mug contains 330 milliliters of water.

    a. How much water is in the 3 mugs?
    b. How much water was there to start with?

Give your answer in liters and milliliters.

4. A ball of yarn is cut into 4 pieces.
Each piece is 65 centimeters long.

    a. How long was the ball of yarn?
    b. How much yarn is left if one piece is given away?

Give your answer in meters and centimeters.

5.   Ricardo wants to find the distance from his house to the library.

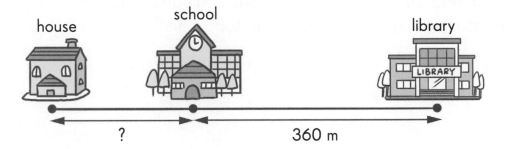

house   school   library

?   360 m

The distance from his house to the library is 3 times the distance from his house to the school.

a.   What is the distance from Ricardo's house to the school?

b.   What is the distance between his house and the library?

6. A butcher has a large piece of beef. He cuts and sells 6 portions.
Each has a mass of 10 kilograms. He has 2 kilograms left.
Find the total mass of beef the butcher had at first.

7. There is 141 milliliters of water in a mug.
Rachel spills 45 milliliters of water from the mug.
She then pours the remaining water equally into 4 cups.
How much water is in each cup?

8.   Mrs. Vance buys 710 grams of strawberries.
She has 210 grams of strawberries left after making
5 glasses of strawberry smoothie.
How many grams of strawberries does she use for a glass?

9.   In a story, a tortoise and a hare take part in a race.
They have to run up and down the same hill.
The distance from the foot to the top of the hill is 996 meters.
The hare takes a nap after running 578 meters.
How much further must the hare run to complete the race?
Give your answer in kilometers and meters.

10. Six glasses of water can fill a bottle.
Two bottles of water can fill a pitcher.
The pitcher can hold 600 milliliters of water.
How much water can a glass hold?

Put On Your Thinking Cap!

Challenging Practice

Ron puts two sticks into the ground as shown.
Stick B is 10 centimeters longer than Stick A.
What is the length of Stick A that is above the ground?

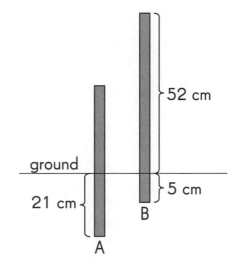

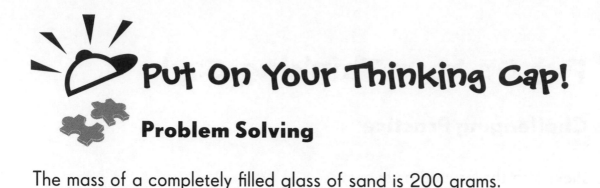

Put On Your Thinking Cap!

Problem Solving

The mass of a completely filled glass of sand is 200 grams.
When half of the sand is poured out, the total mass of
the glass of sand is 120 grams.
What is the mass of the empty glass?

Cumulative Review

for Chapters 10 to 12

Concepts and Skills

Read the scale. *(Lesson 11.3)*

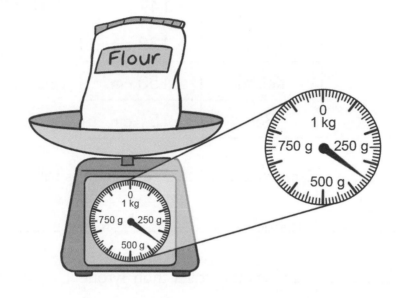

1.   The mass of the bag of flour is _____ grams.

Write *true* or *false*.

2.   6,016 meters is the same as 6 meters 16 centimeters. *(Lesson 11.1)* _____

3.   7 kilograms 3 grams is the same as 7,030 grams. *(Lesson 11.3)*   _____

4.   4 liters 250 milliliters is the same as 4,250 milliliters. *(Lesson 11.4)* _____

Fill in the blanks.

The table shows the height of five students. *(Lesson 11.1)*

Student	Height
Tiva	143 cm
Britney	149 cm
Tyrone	138 cm
Keisha	150 cm
Ben	151 cm

5. Britney is _____ meter _____ centimeters tall.

6. The height of the tallest student is _____ meter _____ centimeters.

7. Keisha is _____ centimeters taller than Tyrone.

8. Which bag has a different mass from the others? *(Lesson 11.3)*

Bag A   Bag B   Bag C

Bag _____ has a different mass from the other two.

Name: _____   **Date:** _____

Fill in the blanks. *(Lesson 11.4)*

Each container is completely filled with water.
The water is emptied into measuring cups.

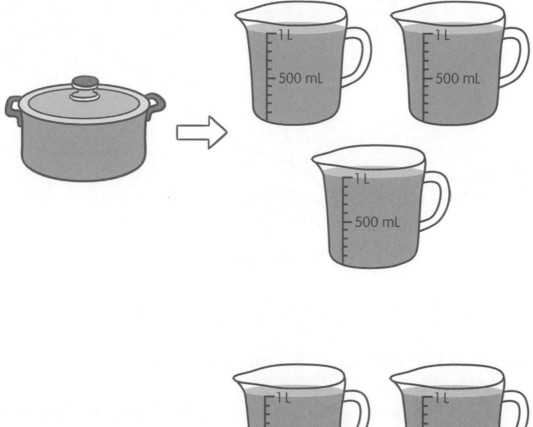

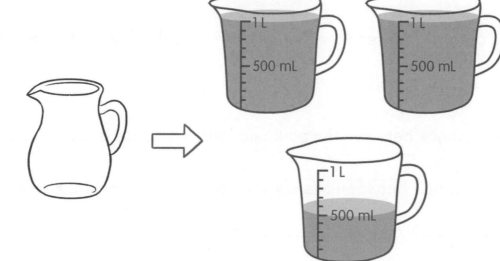

9. The _____ has the greater capacity.

10. The container with the greater capacity can hold _____ milliliters of water.

Look at the picture.
Complete. *(Lesson 11.2)*

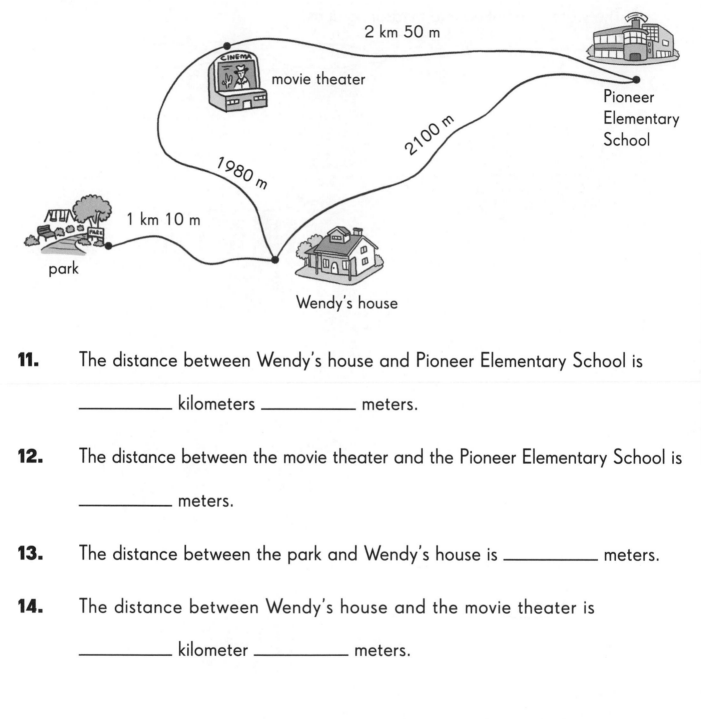

11. The distance between Wendy's house and Pioneer Elementary School is

_____ kilometers _____ meters.

12. The distance between the movie theater and the Pioneer Elementary School is

_____ meters.

13. The distance between the park and Wendy's house is _____ meters.

14. The distance between Wendy's house and the movie theater is

_____ kilometer _____ meters.

Problem Solving

Solve. Show your work.

15.   Hayley is saving for a book that costs $19.50.
She has saved $7.85.
How much more does she need to save?

16.   The table shows the amount of money Tim saved for three months.

January	February	March	Total
$10.55	$15.70	?	$50

How much did Tim save in March? $_____

Solve. Show your work.

17. Nigel has 13 quarters.
Madi has $6.85.
How much money do they have in all?

18. The mass of 3 tomatoes and a squash is 730 grams.
The mass of the squash is 430 grams. What is the mass
of one tomato?

Solve. Show your work.

19. A sparrow flies 256 meters. An eagle flies three times as far as the sparrow. The distance flown by the eagle is twice that of the pigeon. How far does the pigeon fly?

20. An equal amount of lemonade is poured into 3 cups.
The pitcher has 40 milliliters left in it.
Each cup has 325 milliliters of lemonade.
How much lemonade was in the pitcher at first?
Express your answer in liters and milliliters.

Solve. Show your work.

21. Elle had $85.30.
After buying two of these items, she has $25.75 left.

a. How much did the two items cost?

b. Which two items did she buy?

Do you need an exact answer or an estimate to solve this?

bicycle $ 45

jacket $14.55

cap $ 10

watch $30·25

Chapter 13 Bar Graphs and Line Plots

Practice 1   Making Bar Graphs with Scales

The picture graph shows the number of each kind of kite some students made after school.

Kites Made by the Students

Fish	🪁 🪁 🪁 🪁 🪁 🪁
Round	🪁 🪁 🪁 🪁
Butterfly	🪁 🪁 🪁 🪁 🪁
Bird	🪁 🪁 🪁 🪁 🪁 🪁 🪁

Key: Each 🪁 stands for 1 kite.

Talya used the data from the picture graph to make a bar graph. She used a scale of 2.

Help Talya complete the bar graph.

1.

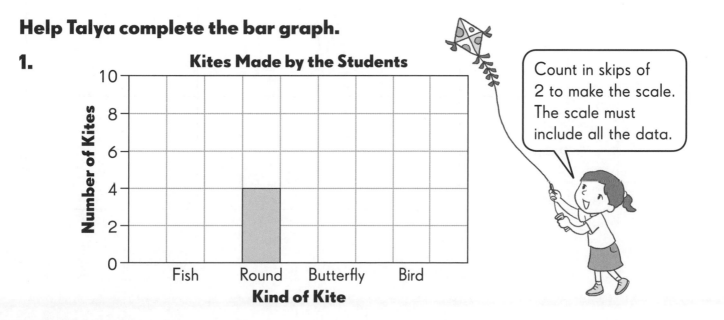

Count in skips of 2 to make the scale. The scale must include all the data.

Alice went to a bird park and saw 5 kinds of birds.
She recorded the number of each kind of bird she saw in a tally chart.

Complete the tally chart.

2.

Birds Alice Saw at the Bird Park

Name of Bird	Tally	Number of Birds
Eagle	~~IIII~~ ~~IIII~~ II	
Ostrich		2
Parrot		6
Peacock	IIII	
Penguin		14

Complete the bar graph to show the birds Alice saw.

3.

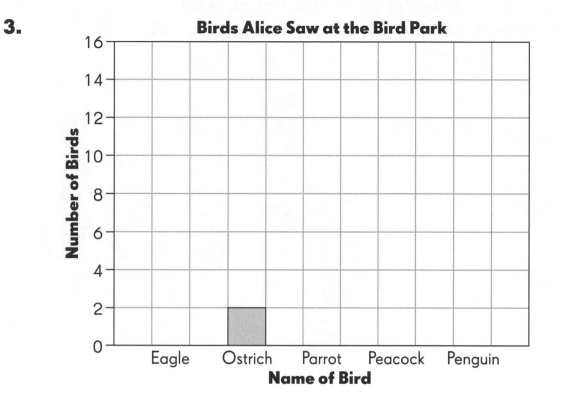

Birds Alice Saw at the Bird Park

Answer each question.
Use the data in the bar graph.

4.   The scale shows skip counts of _____

5.   What is the greatest number on the vertical axis? _____
        Explain why.

        _____

        _____

        _____

Joy and her friends are making animal masks.
Count the number of each type of mask they have made.
Complete the tally chart and bar graph on page 65.

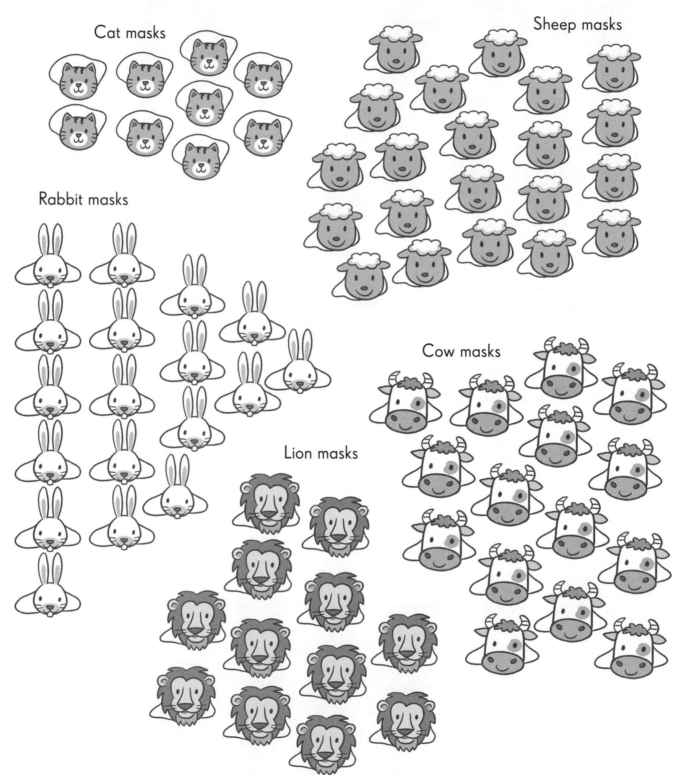

Cat masks

Sheep masks

Rabbit masks

Cow masks

Lion masks

Complete.

6.
Masks Made by Joy and Her Friends

Kind of Mask	Tally	Number of Masks
Cat mask		
Sheep mask		
Cow mask		
Rabbit mask		
Lion mask		

Complete the bar graph. Use the data in the tally chart.

7.

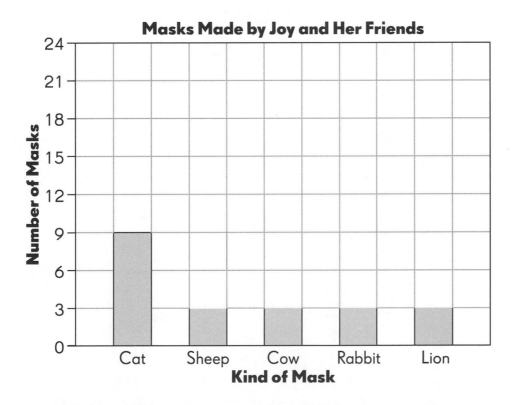

Masks Made by Joy and Her Friends

Answer each question. Use the data in the bar graph.

8. The scale shows skip counts of _____.

9. What is the greatest number on the scale? _____

The picture graph shows the number of points five players scored in a basketball game.

Points Scored by Five Players

Player	Number of Points
Richard	
Paul	
Tom	
Justin	
Leroy	

Key: Each stands for 5 points.

Use the data in the picture graph to complete the bar graph.

10.

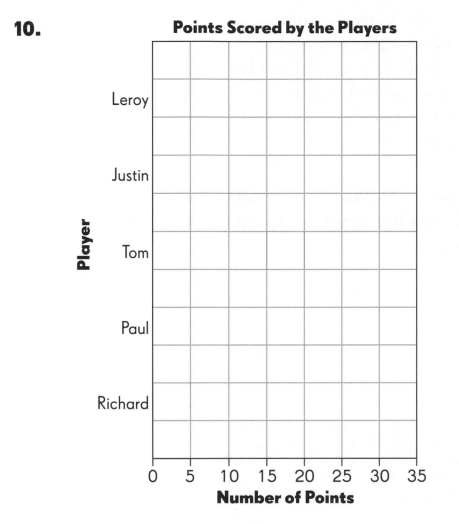

Points Scored by the Players

Player

Leroy

Justin

Tom

Paul

Richard

0   5   10   15   20   25   30   35

Number of Points

Answer each question. Use the data in the bar graph.

11.   The scale shows skip counts of _____.

12.   What is the greatest number on the scale? _____

A survey was carried out to find the favorite activities of third graders.

It was found that ... 10 like to read a book.
12 like to make crafts.
2 times as many children like to play sports as make crafts.
4 fewer children like to visit friends than play sports.

Complete the bar graph to show the favorite activities of third graders. Then fill in the missing activity names in the answer boxes.

13.

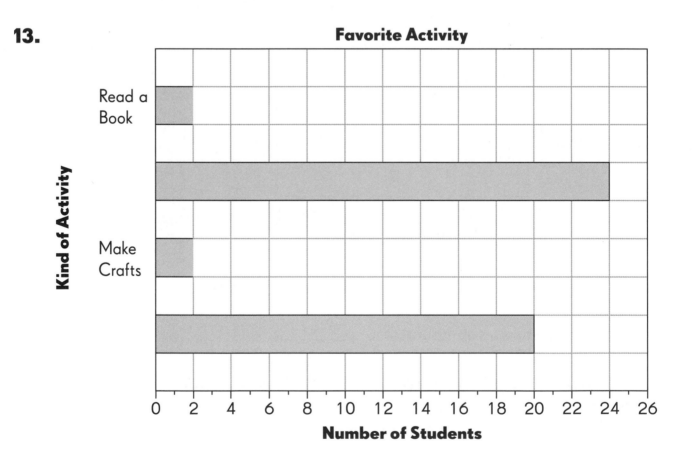

Favorite Activity

Kind of Activity

Read a Book

Make Crafts

Number of Students

Practice 2   Reading and Interpreting Bar Graphs

The bar graph shows the bus tickets that were sold
on Monday, Tuesday, Wednesday, and Thursday.

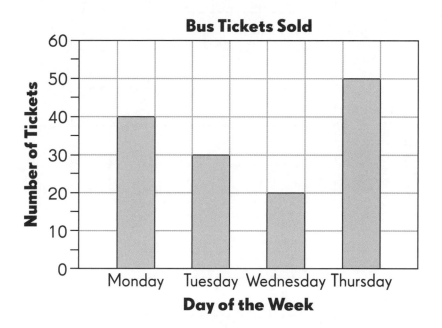

Bus Tickets Sold

Answer each question. Use the data in the bar graph.

1. How many more tickets were sold on Thursday than on Wednesday?

_____ tickets

2. On Thursday, 15 of the tickets sold were for children. How many

tickets sold were for adults? _____ tickets

3. 18 fewer tickets were sold on Friday than on Tuesday. How many

tickets were sold on Friday? _____ tickets

4. The number of tickets sold on Tuesday can be grouped into fives.

How many groups are there? _____ groups

5. How many tickets were sold in all during the four days? _____ tickets

This bar graph shows the number of notebooks that five students have.

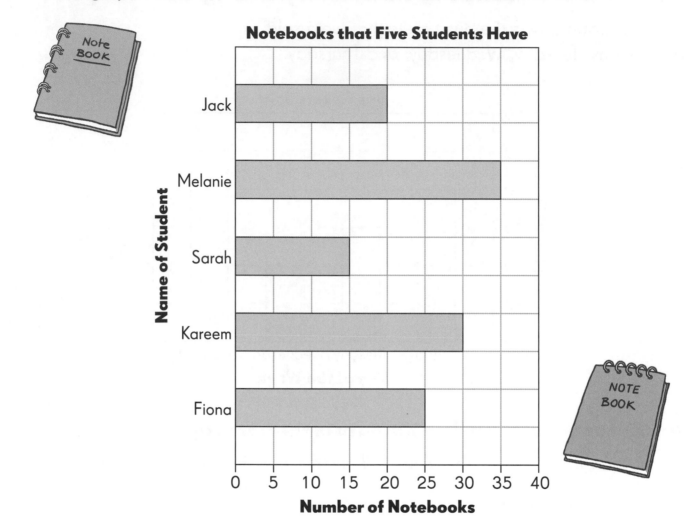

Notebooks that Five Students Have

**Write _T_ for true and _F_ for false in the boxes.
Use the data in the bar graph.**

6. Jack has 20 notebooks.

7. Fiona has 25 notebooks.

8. Melanie has 40 notebooks.

9. Kareem has 5 fewer notebooks than Fiona.

10. Sarah has the least number of notebooks.

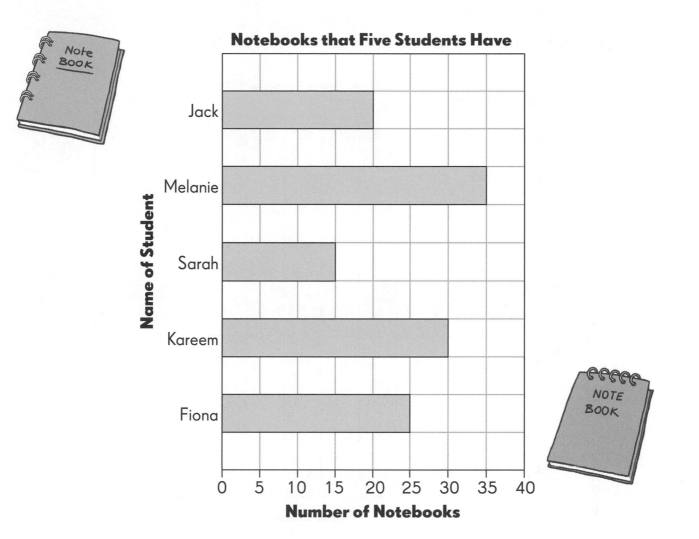

Notebooks that Five Students Have

Answer each question.
Use the data in the bar graph.

11. How many more notebooks does Kareem have than Fiona? _____

12. How many fewer notebooks does Sarah have than Melanie? _____

13. How many notebooks do Melanie and Sarah have altogether? _____

14. Who has twice as many notebooks as Sarah? _____

15. Which two students have a total of 65 notebooks? _____

This bar graph shows the kinds of juices that people like.

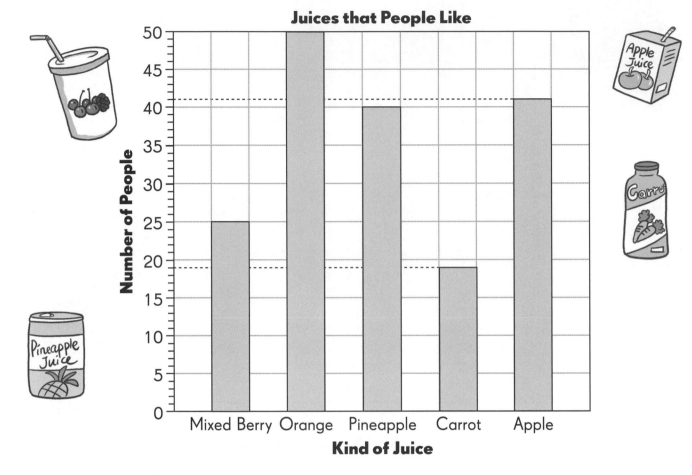

Fill in the blanks.
Use the data in the bar graph.

16. _____ people like mixed berry juice.

17. 19 people like _____ juice.

18. The most popular juice is _____.

19. 16 more people like apple juice than _____ juice.

20. 10 fewer people like _____ juice than the most popular juice.

21. What can you say about orange juice and carrot juice?

_____

_____

Name: _____   Date: _____

Danny sold flowers at the farmer's market.
The bar graph shows the number of flowers he sold.

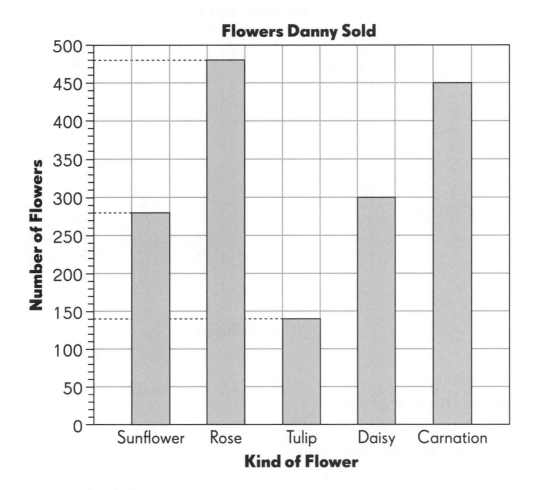

Flowers Danny Sold

Answer each question.
Use the data in the bar graph.

22. How many daisies did Danny sell? _____

23. He sold 150 more carnations than another flower.

Which kind of flower? _____

24. He sold twice as many sunflowers as another kind of flower.

Which kind of flower? _____

25. How many fewer sunflowers than roses were sold? _____

26. He sold a total of 750 of two kinds of flowers.

Which two kinds of flowers could they be? _____

This bar graph shows the subjects that a number of students like.

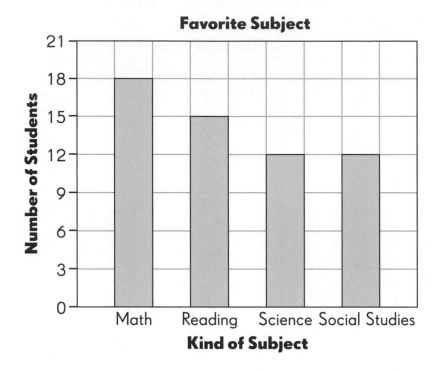

Fill in the blanks.
Use the data in the bar graph.

27. _____ students like math.

28. 3 fewer students like _____ than reading.

29. The number of students who like _____ is equal to the

    number of students who like _____.

30. A total number of 39 students like three kinds of subjects.
    Which three kinds of subjects could they be?

    _____

Practice 3   Line Plots

Amanda surveyed a group of children in a Nature Club to find out their ages. The table below shows the results of her survey.

Ages of Children in Years

Name of Child	Age
José	7
Roger	8
Alex	7
Liza	10
Suki	9
Christy	7
Allie	9
Jeremy	9
Valerie	9
Vilma	8
Jacob	7
Emily	9
Ethan	8
Emma	9
Kayla	10

Amanda made a line plot to show the results of her survey.

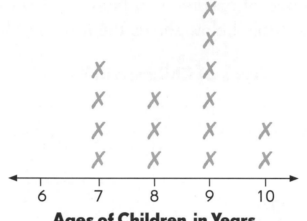

Ages of Children in Years

Answer each question.
Use the data in the line plot.

1. What does each X on the line plot stand for? _____

2. What do the numbers on the number line stand for? _____

3. What is the age of the greatest number of children? _____ years old

4. How many children are aged 6? _____ children

5. What is the age of the oldest child surveyed? _____ years

6. How many children were surveyed in all? _____ children

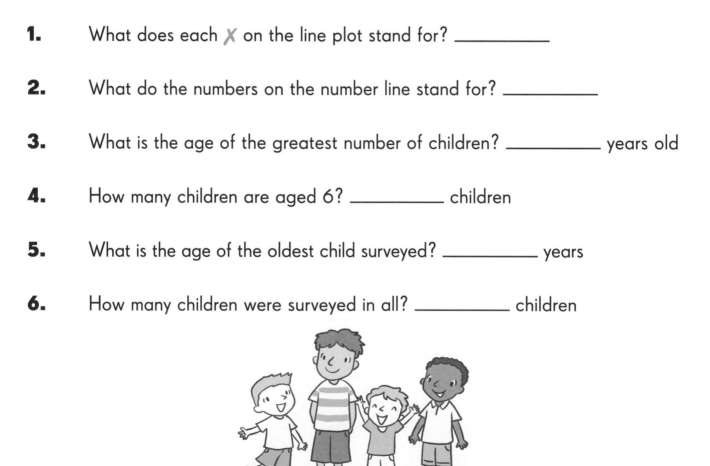

Name: _____   Date: _____

Third graders carried out a survey. They wanted to find the number of children in each of their families. They displayed their results in this line plot.

Number of Children in Each Family

Answer each question.
Use the data in the line plot.

7.   What does each ✗ on the line plot stand for? _____

8.   What do the numbers on the number line stand for? _____

9.   How many families have 2 children? _____ families

10.   How many families have fewer than 4 children? _____ families

11.   What is the greatest number of children in the families surveyed?

_____ children

12.   How many families took part in the survey? _____ families

13.   Did all the families surveyed have children? Answer yes or no. _____

A survey was carried out to find the number of rides a group of children took at Happy Theme Park. The tally chart shows the results of the survey.

Complete the tally chart.

14.

Number of Rides

Number of Rides	Tally	Number of Children
1	////	4
2	//	⬭
3	///	⬭
4	⤧////	⬭
5	///	⬭

Complete the line plot.
Use the data in the tally chart.

15.

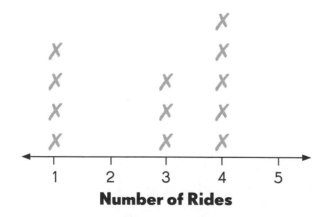

Number of Rides

Answer each question.
Use the data in the line plot.

16.   What does each  on the line plot stand for? _____

17.   What does each number on the number line stand for? _____

18.   How many children take 5 rides? _____ children

19.   How many children take 4 or more rides? _____ children

20.   Which number of rides are taken by the same number of children?

       _____

A baseball team counted the number of home runs each player hit. The results are shown in this table.

Number of Home Runs	0	1	2	3	4
Number of Players	1	2	1	2	3

Complete the table.

21.   **Number of Home Runs**

Number of Home Runs	Number of Players
0	⬚
1	2
2	⬚
3	2
4	3

Fill in the blanks.
Use the data in the table.

22.   The greatest number of home runs hit by any player was _____.

23.   The least number of home runs hit by any player was _____.

Complete the line plot.
Use the data in the table.

24.

Number of Home Runs

Answer each question.
Use the data in the line plot.

25. What does each ✗ on the line plot stand for? _____

26. How many players had 2 home runs? _____ player

27. How many players had more than 1 home run? _____ players

28. What is the greatest number of home runs scored by a single player?

_____ home runs

29. How many players were surveyed in total? _____ players

Tom carried out a survey to find how many raisins there are in boxes of different brands.
He made a line plot to show the results of his survey.

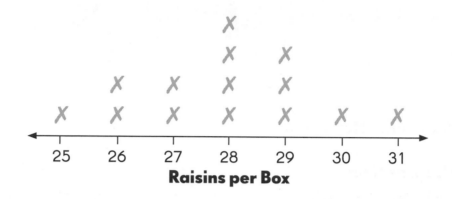

Raisins per Box

Answer each question.
Use the data in the line plot.

30. What is the least number of raisins in a box? _____ raisins

31. What is the greatest number of raisins in a box? _____ raisins

32. Which number of raisins occurs most often? _____ raisins

33. How many boxes contain 28 or more raisins? _____ boxes

34. How many boxes contain fewer than 27 raisins? _____ boxes

35. How many boxes were used in the survey in all? _____ boxes

Math Journal

A survey was carried out to find the scores of students on a 20-minute math quiz.

Number of Questions Right

Name of Student	Number
Sophie	2
Rachel	1
Mimi	1
Kyle	3
Jessica	4
Alex	1
Maria	4
Sue	1
Jane	3

Work in groups to make a line plot.
Use the data in the table.
Follow the steps to help you.

Step 1 Give the line plot a title.

Draw and label the horizontal number line.

Step 2 Draw an X for each student above one number.

Step 3 Check that the number of Xs shows the data in the table.

Answer each question.
Use the data in the line plot.

1. How did you get the least and greatest number on the number line?

_____

_____

_____

2. A survey asks 100 people how many children are in their families. All the people answer 0, 1, 2, 3, or 4. Would a line plot be a good way to show this data? Explain your thinking.

_____

_____

_____

The table shows the number of model trains that 8 children have.
Choose which line plot matches the data.

Name of Student	Katy	Ryan	Noah	Sylvia	Riya	James	Evan	Luke
Number of Model Trains	2	6	3	4	2	5	2	4

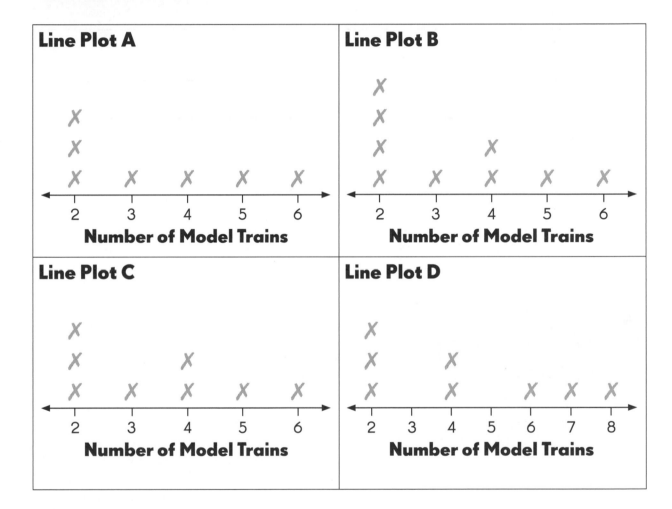

Fill in the blank.
Use the data in the table.

3.   Line plot _____ matches the given data.

Explain the mistakes in the other line plots.

4. _____

_____

5. _____

_____

6. _____

_____

Put On Your Thinking Cap!

Challenging Practice

Pinocchio's nose grew 2 centimeters longer every time he told a lie.
He wanted to stop telling lies and be an honest boy.
He drew a picture graph and a bar graph to check how many fewer
lies he was telling every day.

The picture graph below and the bar graph on page 88 show the length his nose
grew over five days.

Length Pinocchio's Nose Grew over Five Days

Monday	🌱🌱🌱🌱🌱🌱🌱🌱🌱🌱🌱🌱🌱🌱🌱🌱🌱🌱🌱🌱
Tuesday	🌱🌱🌱🌱🌱🌱🌱🌱🌱🌱🌱🌱
Wednesday	🌱🌱🌱🌱🌱🌱🌱🌱🌱🌱🌱
Thursday	🌱🌱🌱🌱🌱🌱🌱🌱🌱
Friday	🌱🌱🌱🌱🌱🌱

Key: Each 🌱 stands for 2 centimeters.

© Marshall Cavendish International (Singapore) Private Limited.

Use the information in the picture graph on page 87.
Fill in the boxes to show the length his nose grew on...

1.

Monday	Tuesday	Wednesday	Thursday	Friday

cm   cm   cm   cm   cm

Complete the bar graph for Friday.

2.

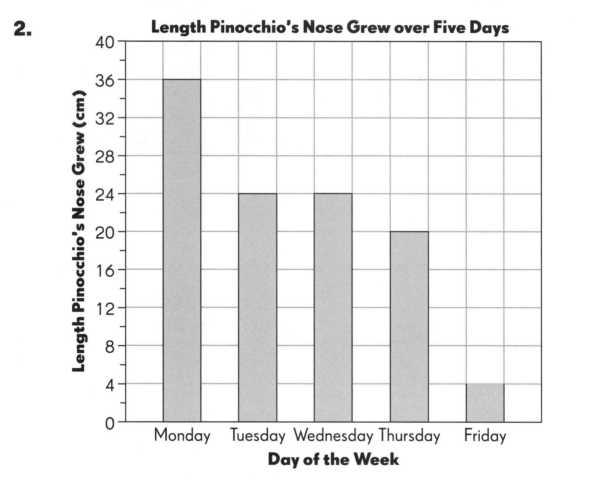

Answer each question.
Use the data in the bar graph.

3.   On which day did his nose grow by 24 centimeters? _____

4.   For which day is the bar graph incorrectly drawn? _____

5.   How much longer does his nose grow on Tuesday than on Friday?

_____

Put On Your Thinking Cap!

Problem Solving

Study each set of data carefully.
Decide which graph would best represent each data.

Fill in the blanks with *Picture Graph*, *Bar Graph*, or *Line Plot*.

The table below shows the number of visitors at the art museum during six months.
Erin wants to show the difference in the number of visitors for the months of February and April.

Month	Number of Visitors
January	230
February	80
March	340
April	400
May	420
June	540

> The sample is large.
> Erin wants to compare the data.

_____

Alisha wants to know which snack is most popular with third graders.
She asks some of the third graders and records the data in this table.

Snack	Number of Students
Granola Bar	12
Strawberry Yogurt	18
Fruit Cup	24
Raisins	30

_____

© Marshall Cavendish International (Singapore) Private Limited.

A group of students took part in a math competition.
At the end of the competition, Mr. Stephenson wanted to
show how many games his students won.
He recorded his findings in this table.

Number of Games Won	Number of Students
0	2
1	6
2	4
3	3
4	1

 Fractions

Practice 1   Understanding Fractions

Find the fractions that make a whole.

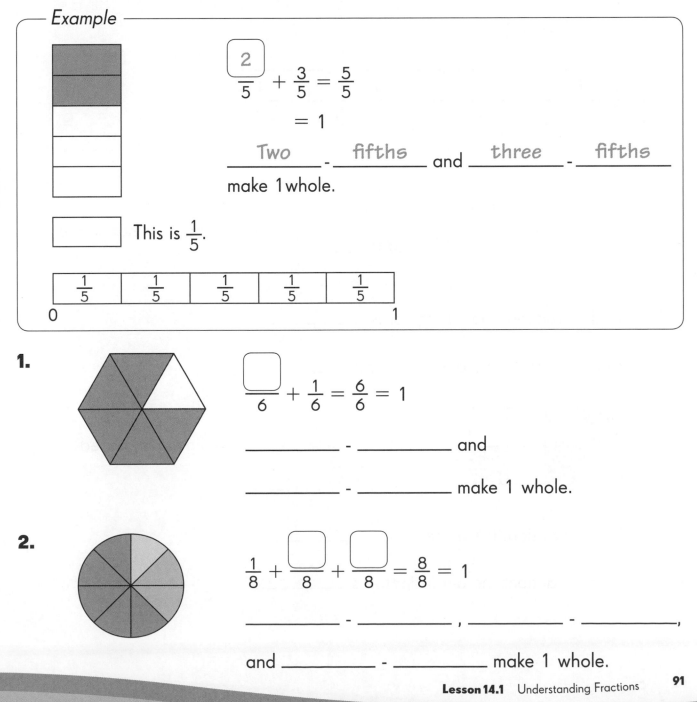

Example

$$\boxed{\frac{2}{5}} + \frac{3}{5} = \frac{5}{5}$$

$$= 1$$

___Two___ - ___fifths___ and ___three___ - ___fifths___
make 1 whole.

This is $\frac{1}{5}$.

| $\frac{1}{5}$ | $\frac{1}{5}$ | $\frac{1}{5}$ | $\frac{1}{5}$ | $\frac{1}{5}$ |

0   1

1.

$$\frac{\boxed{}}{6} + \frac{1}{6} = \frac{6}{6} = 1$$

_____ - _____ and

_____ - _____ make 1 whole.

2.

$$\frac{1}{8} + \frac{\boxed{}}{8} + \frac{\boxed{}}{8} = \frac{8}{8} = 1$$

_____ - _____ , _____ - _____ ,

and _____ - _____ make 1 whole.

Name the numerator and denominator.

Example

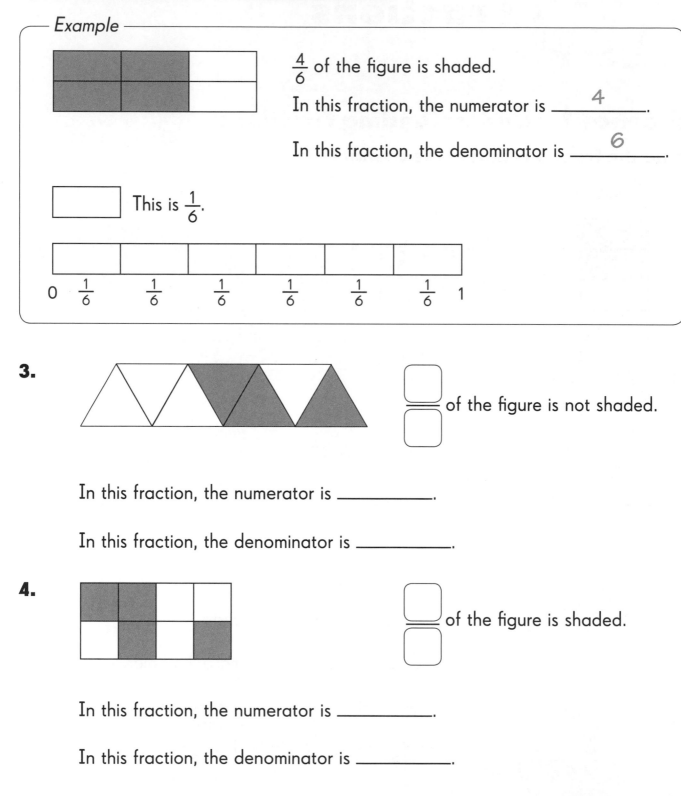

$\frac{4}{6}$ of the figure is shaded.

In this fraction, the numerator is ___4___.

In this fraction, the denominator is ___6___.

This is $\frac{1}{6}$.

0   $\frac{1}{6}$ $\frac{1}{6}$ $\frac{1}{6}$ $\frac{1}{6}$ $\frac{1}{6}$ $\frac{1}{6}$ 1

3.

☐/☐ of the figure is not shaded.

In this fraction, the numerator is _____.

In this fraction, the denominator is _____.

4.

☐/☐ of the figure is shaded.

In this fraction, the numerator is _____.

In this fraction, the denominator is _____.

Practice 2   Understanding Equivalent Fractions

Shade the part(s) to show fractions equivalent to $\frac{1}{4}$.
Write the fractions.

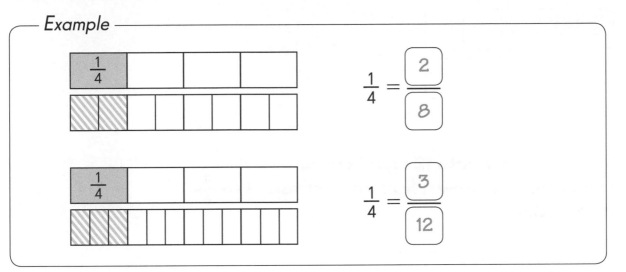

Example

$\frac{1}{4} = \dfrac{2}{8}$

$\frac{1}{4} = \dfrac{3}{12}$

Shade the part(s) to show fractions equivalent to $\frac{1}{5}$.
Write the fractions.

1.

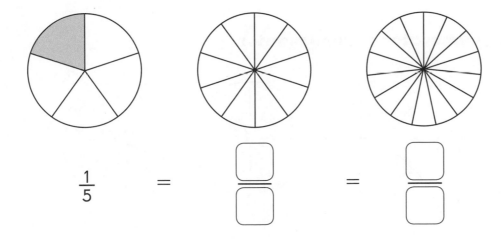

$\dfrac{1}{5} \quad = \quad \dfrac{\Box}{\Box} \quad = \quad \dfrac{\Box}{\Box}$

Divide the second bar into 10 equal parts.
Shade the part(s) to show a fraction equivalent to $\frac{2}{5}$.
Write the fraction.

2.

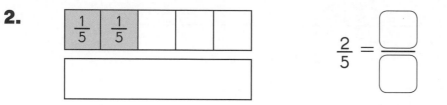

$$\frac{2}{5} = \frac{\boxed{}}{\boxed{}}$$

Divide the second bar into 12 equal parts.
Shade the part(s) to show a fraction equivalent to $\frac{5}{6}$.
Write the fraction.

3.

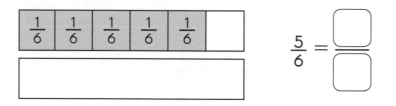

$$\frac{5}{6} = \frac{\boxed{}}{\boxed{}}$$

Find the missing numerator or denominator.

4.

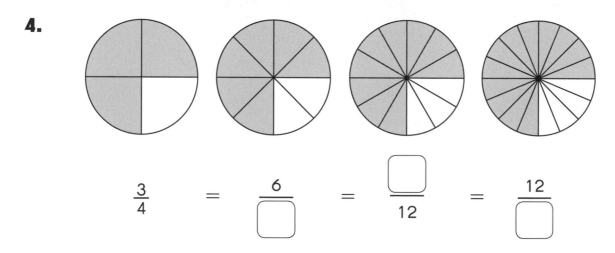

$$\frac{3}{4} = \frac{6}{\boxed{}} = \frac{\boxed{}}{12} = \frac{12}{\boxed{}}$$

Use the number lines to find equivalent fractions.

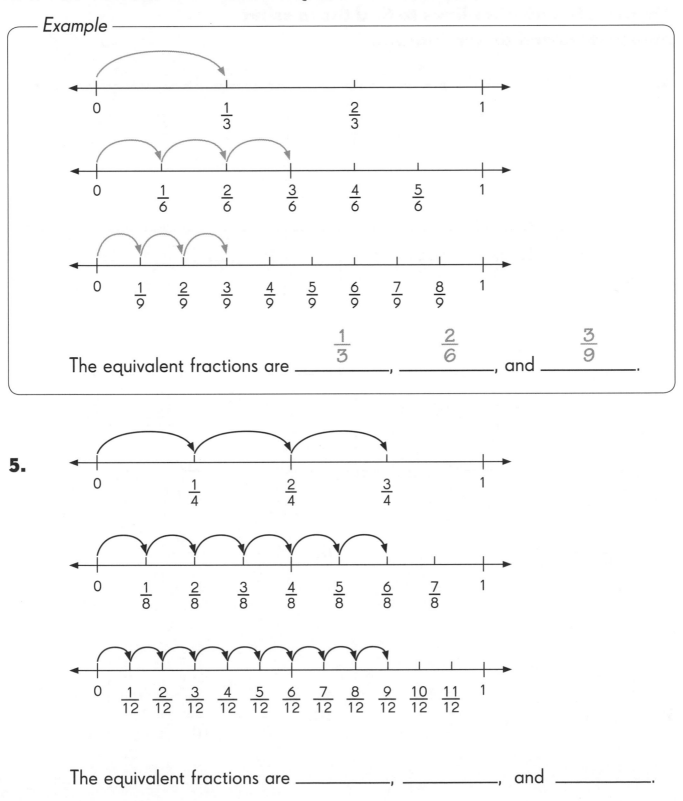

Example

The equivalent fractions are ___$\frac{1}{3}$___, ___$\frac{2}{6}$___, and ___$\frac{3}{9}$___.

5.

The equivalent fractions are _____, _____, and _____.

**Write the missing fractions on the number lines.
Then use the number lines to find the missing
numerators and denominators.**

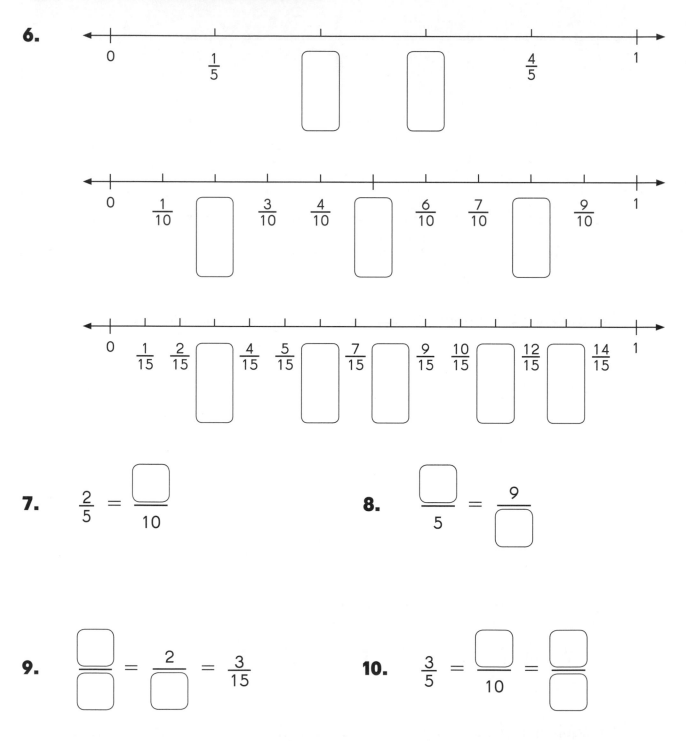

6.

7. $\dfrac{2}{5} = \dfrac{\boxed{}}{10}$

8. $\dfrac{\boxed{}}{5} = \dfrac{9}{\boxed{}}$

9. $\dfrac{\boxed{}}{\boxed{}} = \dfrac{2}{\boxed{}} = \dfrac{3}{15}$

10. $\dfrac{3}{5} = \dfrac{\boxed{}}{10} = \dfrac{\boxed{}}{\boxed{}}$

Practice 3   More Equivalent Fractions

Complete.

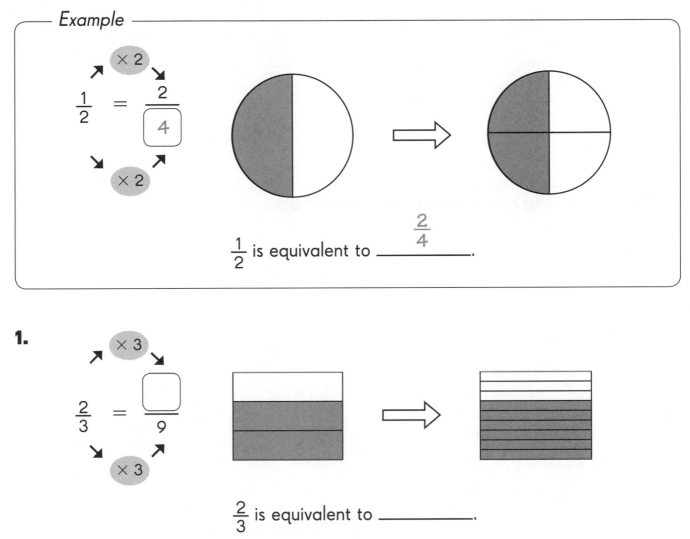

Example

$$\frac{1}{2} = \frac{2}{\boxed{4}}$$

×2 ×2

$\frac{1}{2}$ is equivalent to ___ $\frac{2}{4}$ ___.

1.

$$\frac{2}{3} = \frac{\boxed{}}{9}$$

×3 ×3

$\frac{2}{3}$ is equivalent to _____.

Find the missing numerators and denominators.

2.

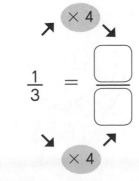

$$\frac{1}{3} = \frac{\boxed{}}{\boxed{}}$$

×4 ×4

3.

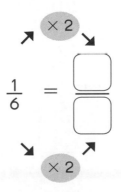

$$\frac{1}{6} = \frac{\boxed{}}{\boxed{}}$$

×2 ×2

Find the missing numerator and denominator.

4.

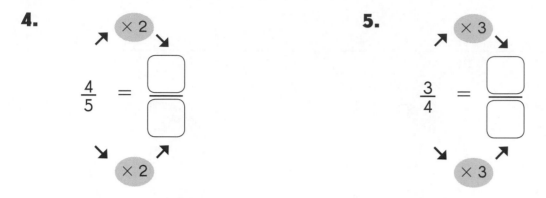

$$\frac{4}{5} = \frac{\boxed{}}{\boxed{}}$$

5.

$$\frac{3}{4} = \frac{\boxed{}}{\boxed{}}$$

Find the missing numerator or denominator.

6. $\dfrac{1}{6} = \dfrac{\boxed{}}{12}$

7. $\dfrac{1}{7} = \dfrac{2}{\boxed{}}$

8. $\dfrac{4}{5} = \dfrac{\boxed{}}{10}$

9. $\dfrac{3}{5} = \dfrac{6}{\boxed{}}$

10. $\dfrac{2}{3} = \dfrac{\boxed{}}{12}$

11. $\dfrac{3}{4} = \dfrac{12}{\boxed{}}$

12. $\dfrac{1}{4} = \dfrac{\boxed{}}{8} = \dfrac{3}{\boxed{}}$

13. $\dfrac{2}{7} = \dfrac{\boxed{}}{14} = \dfrac{\boxed{}}{21}$

14. $\dfrac{2}{5} = \dfrac{6}{\boxed{}} = \dfrac{12}{\boxed{}}$

15. $\dfrac{3}{\boxed{}} = \dfrac{6}{12} = \dfrac{\boxed{}}{24}$

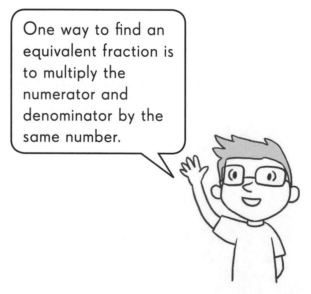

One way to find an equivalent fraction is to multiply the numerator and denominator by the same number.

Complete.

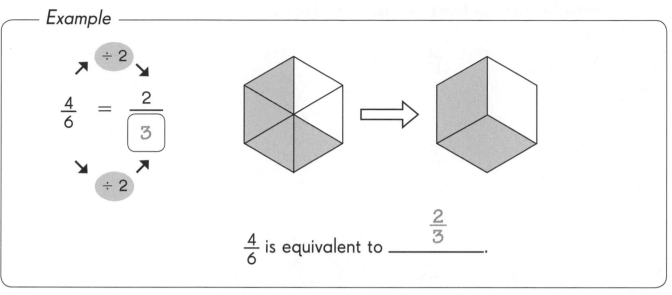

Example

$$\frac{4}{6} = \frac{2}{\boxed{3}}$$

$\frac{4}{6}$ is equivalent to $\frac{2}{3}$____.

16.

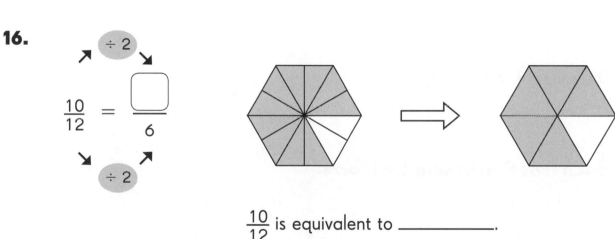

$$\frac{10}{12} = \frac{\boxed{}}{6}$$

$\frac{10}{12}$ is equivalent to _____.

Find the missing numerator or denominator.

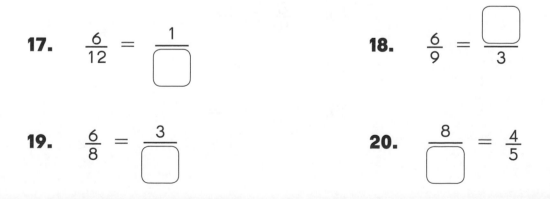

17. $\frac{6}{12} = \frac{1}{\boxed{}}$

18. $\frac{6}{9} = \frac{\boxed{}}{3}$

19. $\frac{6}{8} = \frac{3}{\boxed{}}$

20. $\frac{8}{\boxed{}} = \frac{4}{5}$

Complete the equivalent fractions.
Then write each fraction in simplest form.

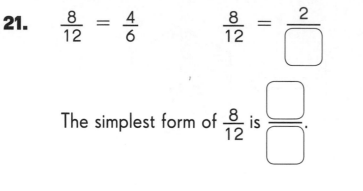

21. $\frac{8}{12} = \frac{4}{6}$ $\frac{8}{12} = \frac{2}{\boxed{}}$

The simplest form of $\frac{8}{12}$ is $\frac{\boxed{}}{\boxed{}}$.

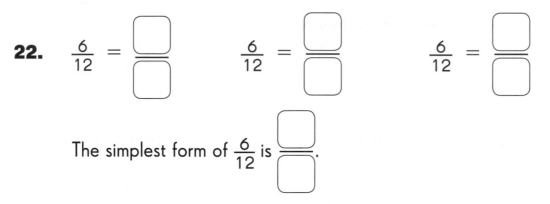

22. $\frac{6}{12} = \frac{\boxed{}}{\boxed{}}$ $\frac{6}{12} = \frac{\boxed{}}{\boxed{}}$ $\frac{6}{12} = \frac{\boxed{}}{\boxed{}}$

The simplest form of $\frac{6}{12}$ is $\frac{\boxed{}}{\boxed{}}$.

Write each fraction in simplest form.

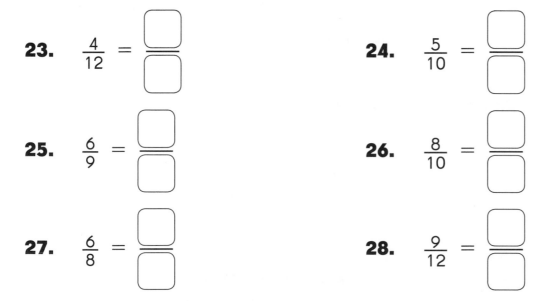

23. $\frac{4}{12} = \frac{\boxed{}}{\boxed{}}$ **24.** $\frac{5}{10} = \frac{\boxed{}}{\boxed{}}$

25. $\frac{6}{9} = \frac{\boxed{}}{\boxed{}}$ **26.** $\frac{8}{10} = \frac{\boxed{}}{\boxed{}}$

27. $\frac{6}{8} = \frac{\boxed{}}{\boxed{}}$ **28.** $\frac{9}{12} = \frac{\boxed{}}{\boxed{}}$

Practice 4   Comparing Fractions

Compare the fractions.

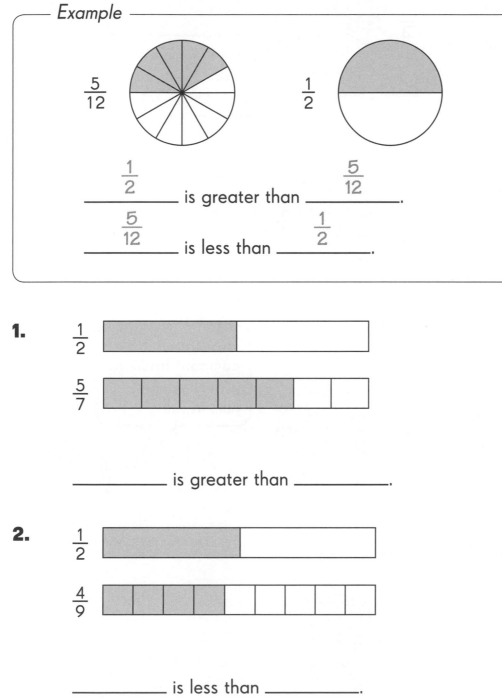

Example

$\frac{5}{12}$ $\frac{1}{2}$

_____ $\frac{1}{2}$ is greater than _____ $\frac{5}{12}$.

_____ $\frac{5}{12}$ is less than _____ $\frac{1}{2}$.

1. $\frac{1}{2}$

$\frac{5}{7}$

_____ is greater than _____.

2. $\frac{1}{2}$

$\frac{4}{9}$

_____ is less than _____.

Compare the fractions.

3.

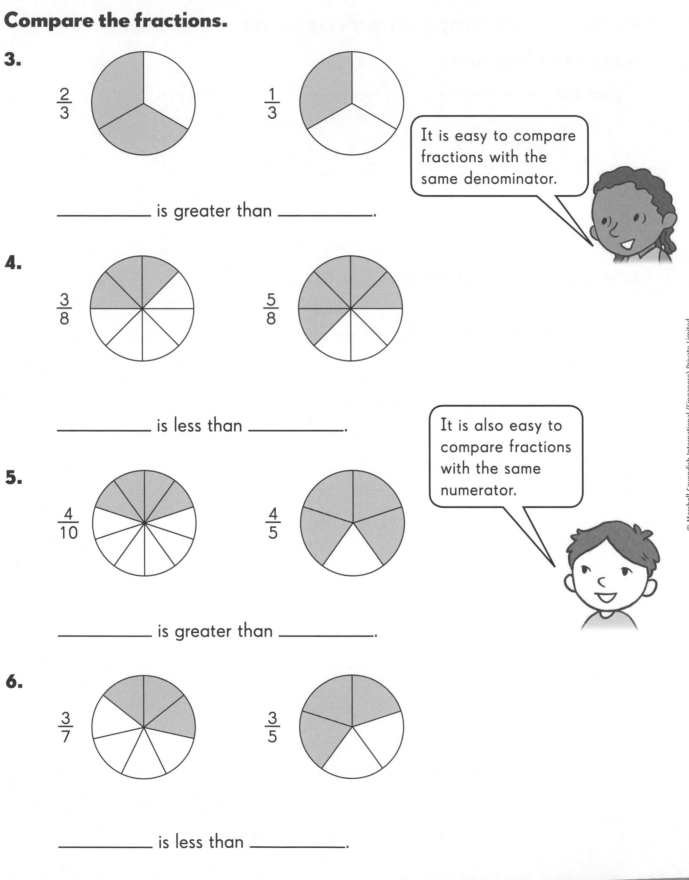

$\frac{2}{3}$ $\frac{1}{3}$

It is easy to compare fractions with the same denominator.

_____ is greater than _____.

4.

$\frac{3}{8}$ $\frac{5}{8}$

_____ is less than _____.

It is also easy to compare fractions with the same numerator.

5.

$\frac{4}{10}$ $\frac{4}{5}$

_____ is greater than _____.

6.

$\frac{3}{7}$ $\frac{3}{5}$

_____ is less than _____.

Name: _____   Date: _____

Compare the fractions.

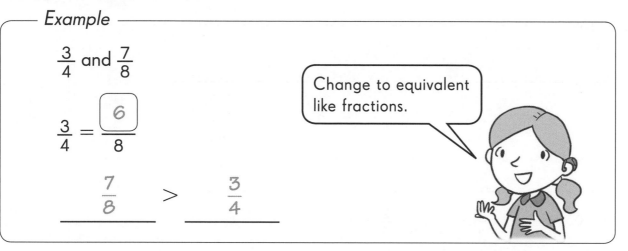

$\frac{3}{4}$ and $\frac{7}{8}$

$\frac{3}{4} = \frac{\boxed{6}}{8}$

Change to equivalent like fractions.

$\frac{7}{8}$ > $\frac{3}{4}$

_____   _____

7. $\frac{7}{9}$ and $\frac{2}{3}$

$\frac{2}{3} = \dfrac{\boxed{}}{\boxed{}}$

_____ < _____

8. $\frac{4}{5}$ and $\frac{1}{2}$

$\frac{4}{5} = \dfrac{\boxed{}}{\boxed{}}$ $\frac{1}{2} = \dfrac{\boxed{}}{\boxed{}}$

_____ > _____

9. $\frac{5}{6}$ and $\frac{1}{4}$

$\frac{5}{6} = \dfrac{\boxed{}}{\boxed{}}$ $\frac{1}{4} = \dfrac{\boxed{}}{\boxed{}}$

_____ < _____

Use the number lines to compare fractions.

Example

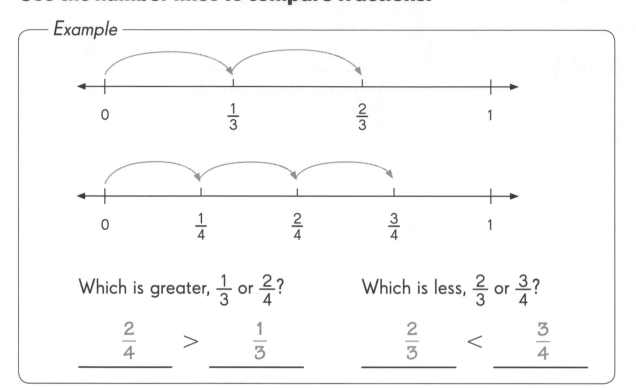

Which is greater, $\frac{1}{3}$ or $\frac{2}{4}$?

$$\frac{2}{4} > \frac{1}{3}$$

Which is less, $\frac{2}{3}$ or $\frac{3}{4}$?

$$\frac{2}{3} < \frac{3}{4}$$

Complete.

10.

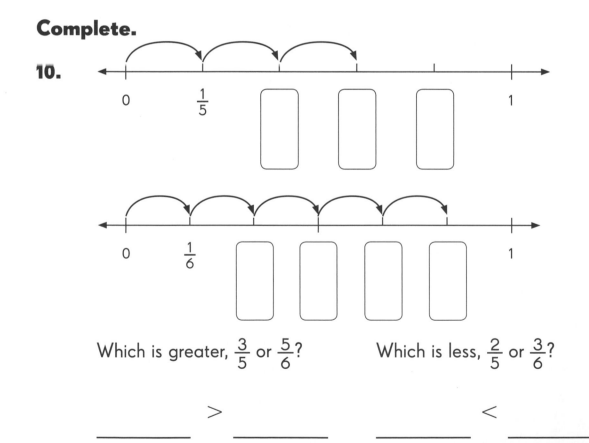

Which is greater, $\frac{3}{5}$ or $\frac{5}{6}$?

$$\underline{} > \underline{}$$

Which is less, $\frac{2}{5}$ or $\frac{3}{6}$?

$$\underline{} < \underline{}$$

Name: ______________________ Date: ______________

Compare. Choose > or <.

Use $\frac{1}{2}$ as a benchmark.

11.

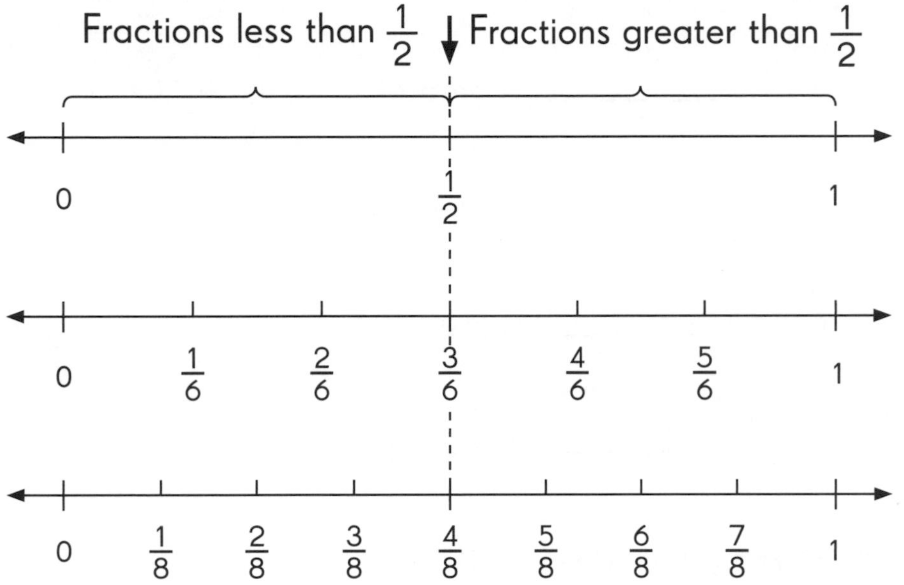

Fractions less than 1/2
Fractions greater than 1/2
0
1/2
1
0
1/6
2/6
3/6
4/6
5/6
1
0
1/8
2/8
3/8
4/8
5/8
6/8
7/8
1

$\frac{4}{6}$ ◯ $\frac{1}{2}$

$\frac{1}{8}$ ◯ $\frac{1}{2}$

So, $\frac{4}{6}$ ◯ $\frac{1}{8}$.

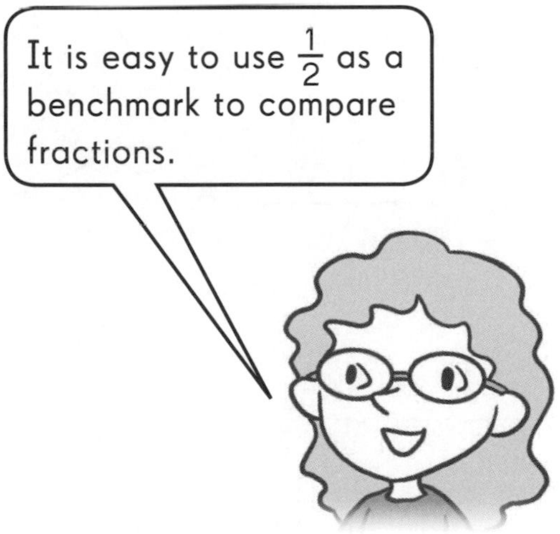

It is easy to use 1/2 as a benchmark to compare fractions.

Compare the fractions. Fill in the blanks.

12. $\frac{4}{7}$ and $\frac{6}{7}$ _____ is greater.

13. $\frac{2}{5}$ and $\frac{2}{10}$ _____ is greater.

14. $\frac{7}{12}$ and $\frac{1}{2}$ _____ is greater.

15. $\frac{5}{11}$ and $\frac{1}{2}$ _____ is less.

16. $\frac{7}{12}$ and $\frac{5}{11}$ _____ is less.

Order the fractions from greatest to least.

Example

$\frac{3}{7}, \frac{3}{8}, \frac{3}{5}$

$\underline{\frac{3}{5}, \frac{3}{7}, \frac{3}{8}}$

The least fraction is the one with the greatest denominator.

17. $\frac{7}{11}, \frac{5}{11}, \frac{11}{11}$

_____

19. $\frac{1}{3}, \frac{1}{2}, \frac{3}{4}$

_____

18. $\frac{2}{3}, \frac{5}{6}, \frac{4}{10}$

Compare each with $\frac{1}{2}$.

$\frac{1}{2} = \frac{\square}{6} = \frac{\square}{10}$

_____

20. $\frac{1}{2}, \frac{2}{3}, \frac{3}{4}$

_____

Practice 5   Fraction as a Whole or Set

Write two fractions for the following whole numbers.

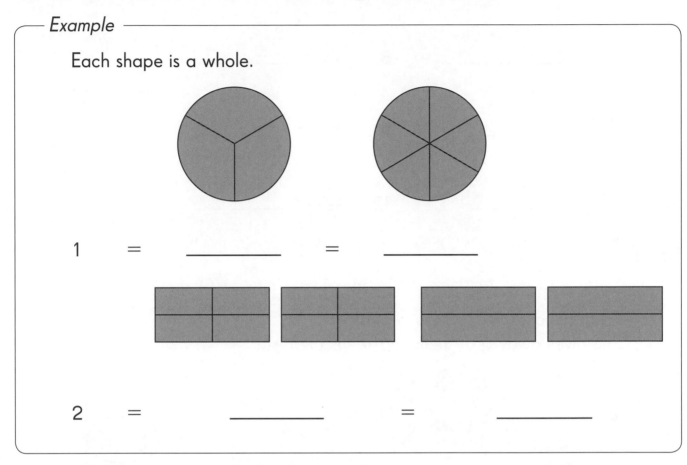

Example

Each shape is a whole.

$1 \ = \ \underline{\hspace{2cm}} \ = \ \underline{\hspace{2cm}}$

$2 \ = \ \underline{\hspace{2cm}} \ = \ \underline{\hspace{2cm}}$

1. $3 = \underline{\hspace{2cm}}; \ 3 = \underline{\hspace{2cm}}$

3. $1 = \underline{\hspace{2cm}}; \ 1 = \underline{\hspace{2cm}}$

3. $7 = \underline{\hspace{2cm}}; \ 7 = \underline{\hspace{2cm}}$

4. $10 = \underline{\hspace{2cm}}; \ 10 = \underline{\hspace{2cm}}$

What numbers are shown by these fractions?

5. $\dfrac{36}{36} = $ _____

6. $\dfrac{18}{3} = $ _____

7. $\dfrac{30}{5} = $ _____

8. $\dfrac{90}{10} = $ _____

9. $\dfrac{16}{2} = $ _____

10. $\dfrac{63}{9} = $ _____

11. $\dfrac{35}{7} = $ _____

12. $\dfrac{32}{8} = $ _____

Solve.

Example

Tabitha makes 9 happy-face pins.
She gives away 6 of them and keeps the rest.

What fraction of the pins does she give away?

Tabitha gives away $\dfrac{6}{9}$ of the pins.

What fraction of the pins does she keep?

She keeps $\dfrac{3}{9}$ of the pins.

$\dfrac{6}{9} = \dfrac{2}{3}$

$\dfrac{3}{9} = \dfrac{1}{3}$

Name: _____   **Date:** _____

Solve.

13.   Shawn paints 2 out of 5 model trucks green.
He paints the rest brown.
Color the trucks to help you.

a.   What fraction of the trucks are green?

b.   What fraction of the trucks are brown?

14.   Shawn buys more trucks. He now has 20 trucks.
He paints them in the same fractional parts as before.
Color the trucks to help you.

a.   What fraction of the trucks are green?

b.   What fraction of the trucks are brown?

Solve.

15.   What fraction of the buttons are gray?

16.   What fraction of the buttons are not gray?

17.   What fraction of the buttons have 3 holes?

18.   What fraction of the buttons are white with 2 holes?

19.   What fraction of the buttons are white with 4 holes?

20.   What fraction of the buttons are round?

21.   Find $\frac{3}{4}$ of 20.

$\frac{1}{4}$ of 20 = ☐

$\frac{2}{4}$ of 20 = ☐

So, $\frac{3}{4}$ of 20 = ☐.

© Marshall Cavendish International (Singapore) Private Limited.

Solve.

22. Serena buys 24 breakfast bars.
$\frac{3}{4}$ of them are blueberry.

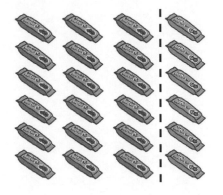

How many blueberry breakfast bars does Serena buy?

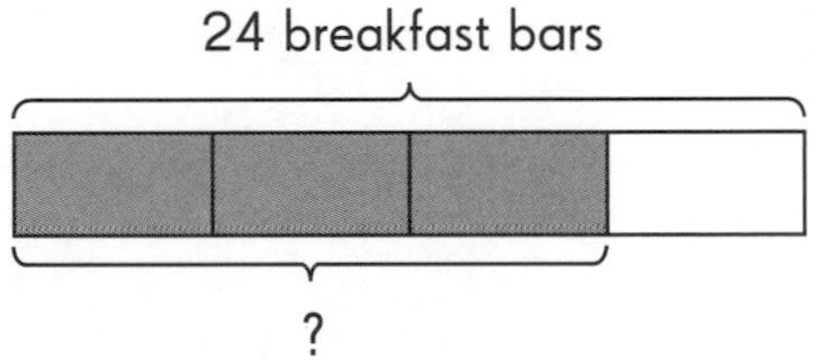

24 breakfast bars

?

4 units → ☐

1 unit → ☐ ÷ ☐

= ☐

3 units → ☐ × ☐

= ☐

Serena buys ☐ blueberry breakfast bars.

Put On Your Thinking Cap!

Challenging Practice

1. Write a fraction with a denominator of 9.

   The fraction should be less than $\frac{1}{2}$.

Mark the number lines to help you.

2.

   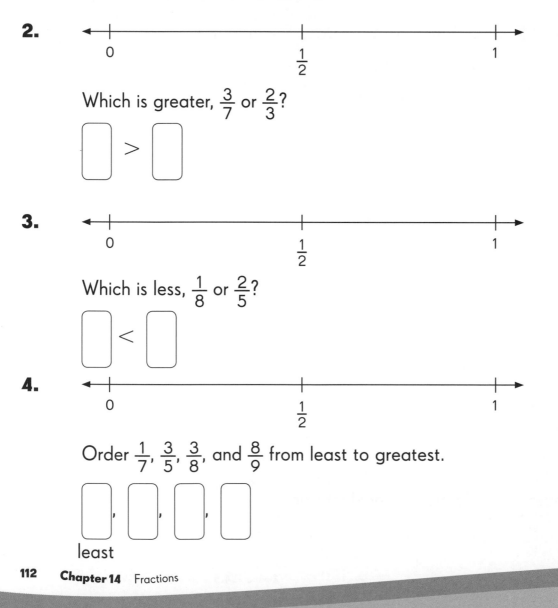

   Which is greater, $\frac{3}{7}$ or $\frac{2}{3}$?

   ☐ > ☐

3.

   Which is less, $\frac{1}{8}$ or $\frac{2}{5}$?

   ☐ < ☐

4.

   Order $\frac{1}{7}$, $\frac{3}{5}$, $\frac{3}{8}$, and $\frac{8}{9}$ from least to greatest.

   ☐ , ☐ , ☐ , ☐

   least

Put On Your Thinking Cap!

Problem Solving

1. Shade to show a fraction greater than $\frac{1}{4}$ but less than $\frac{1}{2}$.

   Sample:

2. Sam wants to shade $\frac{2}{3}$ of the figure.

   He has already shaded 4 squares.

   How many more squares must he shade?

   Help him shade.

3. Shade the figure to show each fraction below.
Use a different color for shading each fraction.

$$\frac{1}{3}, \frac{1}{4}, \frac{1}{12}$$

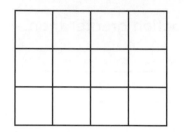

What fraction of the figure is unshaded?

_____ of the figure is unshaded.

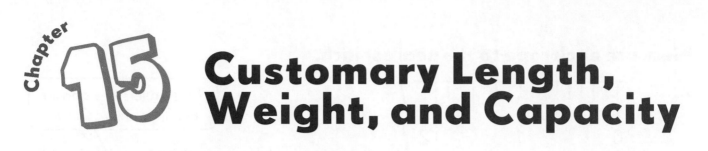

Chapter 15   Customary Length, Weight, and Capacity

Practice 1   Measuring Length

Measure each rope to the nearest inch.

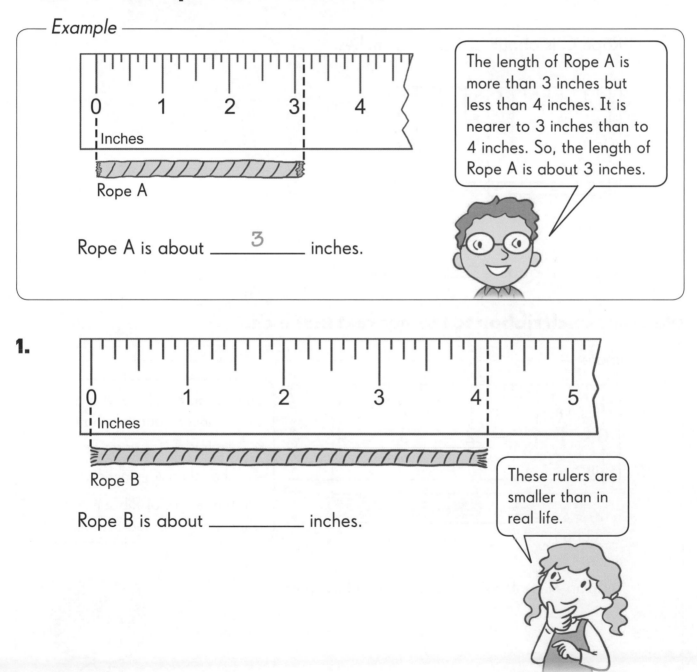

Example

Rope A

The length of Rope A is more than 3 inches but less than 4 inches. It is nearer to 3 inches than to 4 inches. So, the length of Rope A is about 3 inches.

Rope A is about _____3_____ inches.

1.

Rope B

Rope B is about _____ inches.

These rulers are smaller than in real life.

Measure each rope to the nearest inch.

2.

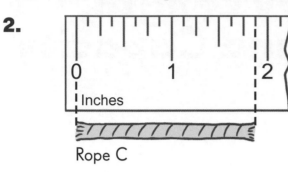

Rope C

These rulers are smaller than in real life.

Rope C is about _____ inches.

3.

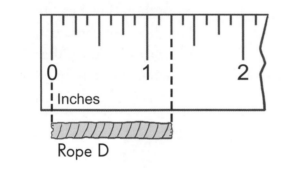

Rope D

Rope D is about _____ inch.

Measure each ribbon to the nearest half inch.

─ *Example* ─

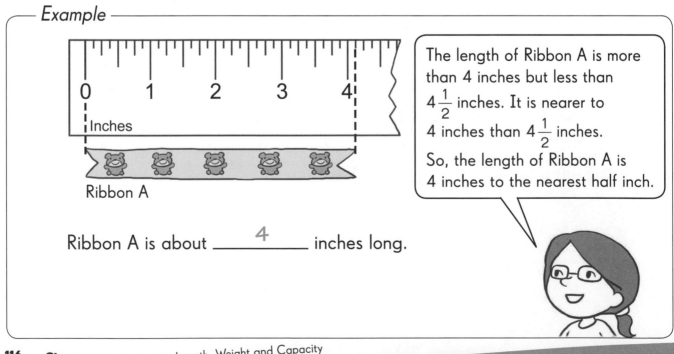

Ribbon A

The length of Ribbon A is more than 4 inches but less than $4\frac{1}{2}$ inches. It is nearer to 4 inches than $4\frac{1}{2}$ inches. So, the length of Ribbon A is 4 inches to the nearest half inch.

Ribbon A is about ____4____ inches long.

4.

Ribbon B

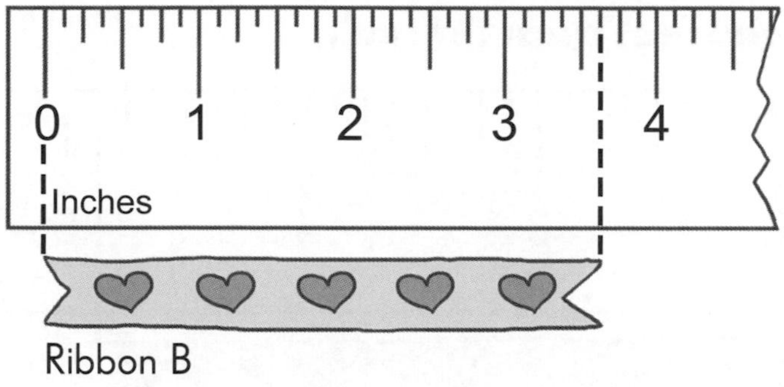

Ribbon B is about _____ inches long.

These rulers are smaller than in real life.

5.

Ribbon C

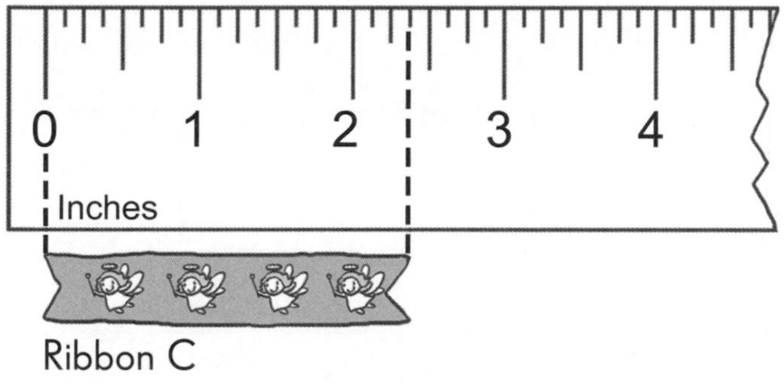

Ribbon C is about _____ inches long.

6.

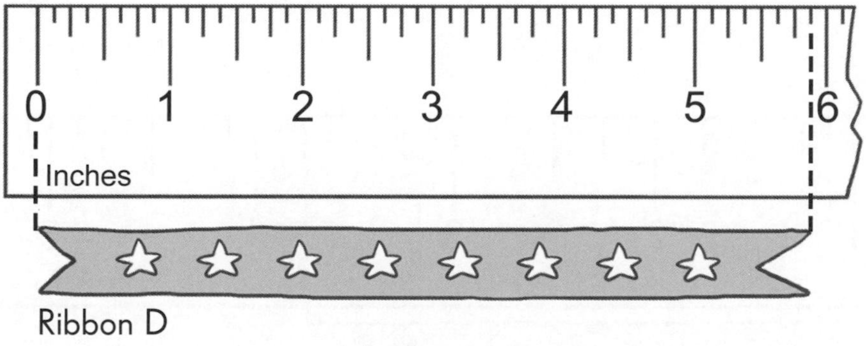

Ribbon D

Ribbon D is about _____ inches long.

Measure each ribbon to the nearest quarter inch.

7.

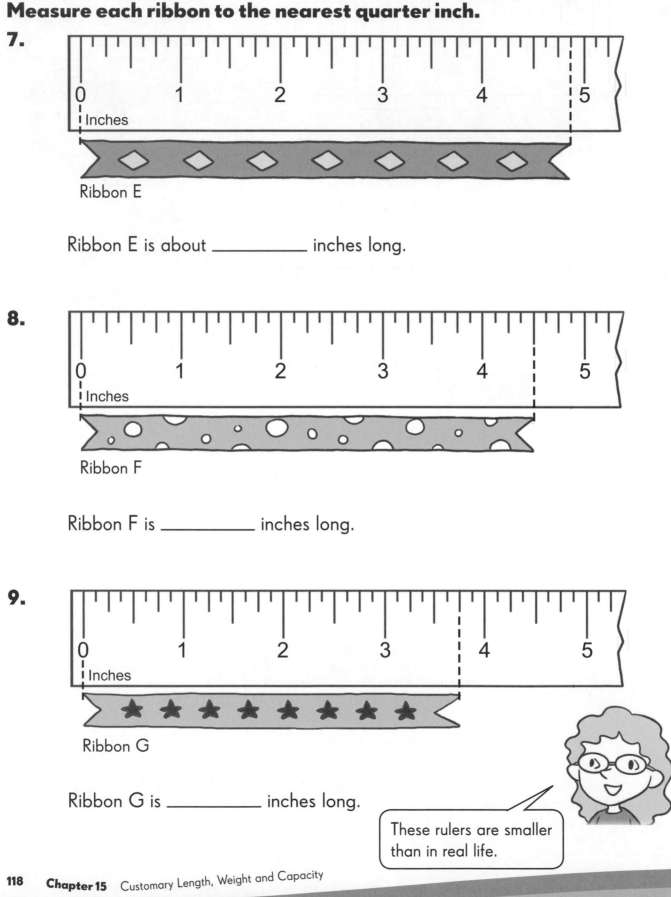

Ribbon E

Ribbon E is about _____ inches long.

8.

Ribbon F

Ribbon F is _____ inches long.

9.

Ribbon G

Ribbon G is _____ inches long.

These rulers are smaller than in real life.

Name: _____   Date: _____

Estimate the length of each object to the nearest inch.

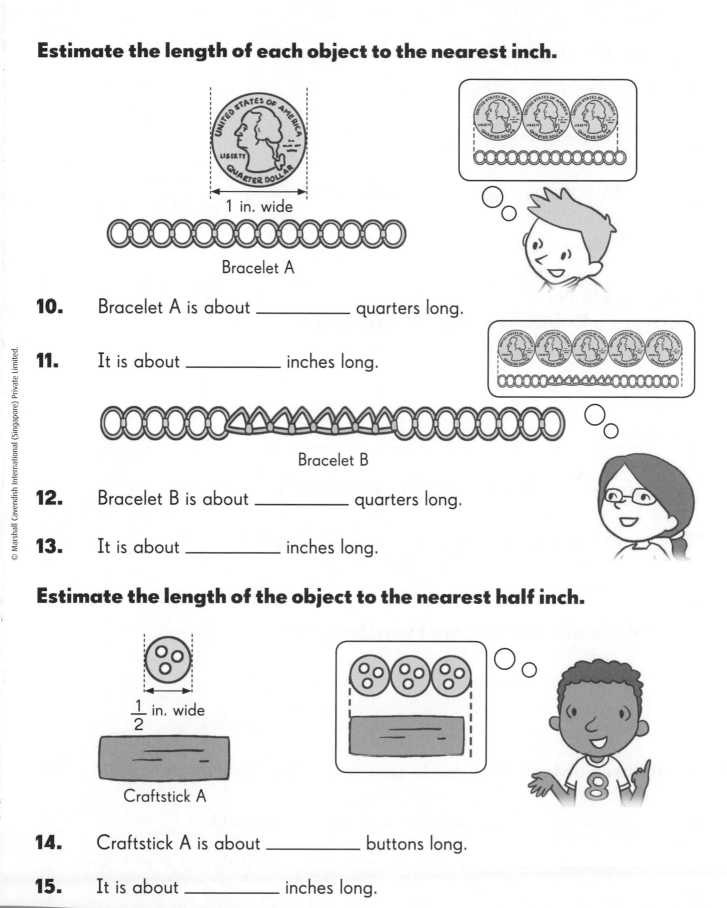

1 in. wide

Bracelet A

10. Bracelet A is about _____ quarters long.

11. It is about _____ inches long.

Bracelet B

12. Bracelet B is about _____ quarters long.

13. It is about _____ inches long.

Estimate the length of the object to the nearest half inch.

$\frac{1}{2}$ in. wide

Craftstick A

14. Craftstick A is about _____ buttons long.

15. It is about _____ inches long.

Estimate the length of each object to the nearest half inch.

Craftstick B

16. Craftstick B is about _____ buttons long.

17. It is about _____ inches long.

Fill in the blanks.
These are a 12-inch ruler and a yardstick.

|← — 1 ft — →|

|← — 1 yd — →|

The ruler and yardstick are smaller than in real life.

Name three objects that are 1 foot long each.

18. The three objects are _____,

_____, and _____.

Name three objects that are 1 yard long each.

19. The three objects are _____,

_____, and _____.

Name three objects that are longer than 1 foot but shorter than 1 yard.

20. _____, _____, and

_____ are longer than 1 foot but shorter than 1 yard.

Sarah is going on a treasure hunt.
She is looking for objects that are about 1 yard long.

Look at the objects she has found.
Then sort them in the table.

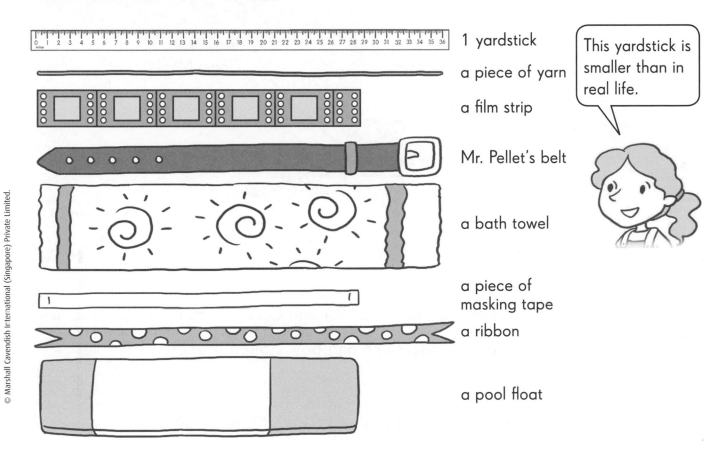

1 yardstick

a piece of yarn

a film strip

Mr. Pellet's belt

a bath towel

a piece of
masking tape

a ribbon

a pool float

This yardstick is smaller than in real life.

21.

Objects less than 1 yard long	Object that are 1 yard long	Objects more than 1 yard long

Complete.
Use the map to help you.

Camp Evergreen

Camp Birch

9 ft

1,760 yd

Camp Maple

1 mile = 1,760 yards
1 yard = 3 feet

5,170 ft

Camp Plane

107 ft

43 yd

Camp Gum

Bay Station

22. The distance between Camp Evergreen and Camp Birch is _____ mile.

23. The distance between Camp Birch and Bay Station is about

_____ mile.

24. The distance between Camp Birch and Camp Maple is _____ yards.

25. Camp _____ is nearer to Bay Station than Camp _____.

26. The distance between Camp Plane and Camp Birch is slightly less than

1,760 _____.

Choose the unit that you would use to measure each.
Write *inch*, *foot*, *yard*, or *mile*.

27. The length of a hiking trail   _____

28. The length of an airplane   _____

29. The height of a teacher   _____

Practice 2   Measuring Weight

Ms. Meyer bought some meat, fruit, and vegetables for her Thanksgiving party.
Read the scales and write the weights.

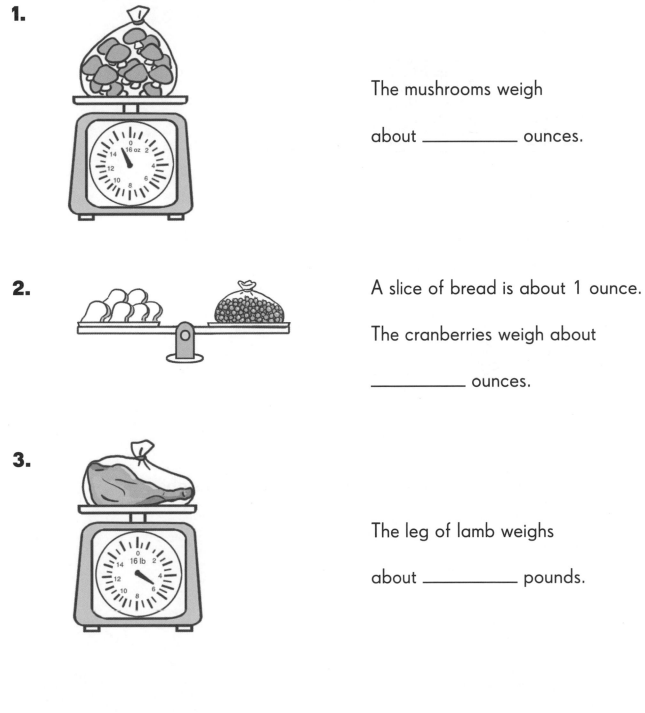

1.

The mushrooms weigh

about _____ ounces.

2.

A slice of bread is about 1 ounce.

The cranberries weigh about

_____ ounces.

3.

The leg of lamb weighs

about _____ pounds.

4.

A loaf of bread is about 1 pound. The tomatoes weigh

about _____ pounds.

5.

The box of cereal weighs

_____ ounces.

Choose the unit that you would use to measure each. Write *ounces*, *pounds*, or *tons*.

6.

A cement truck weighs about

5 _____.

7.

A package of butter weighs about

16 _____.

Name: ______________________ Date: ______________

8.

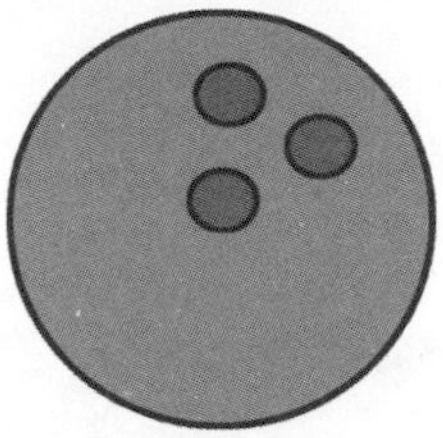

A bowling ball weighs about 9 ________.

9.

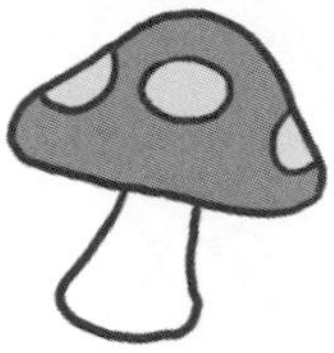

A mushroom weighs about 1 ________.

10.

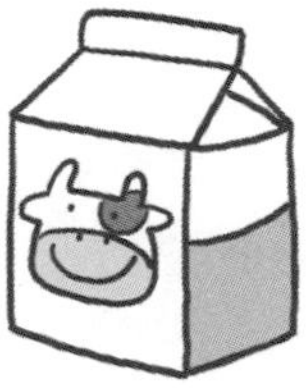

A carton of milk weighs about 12 ________.

Make a guess.
Decide which animals weigh more than 1 ton and which weigh less than 1 ton.
Check your answers using the Internet or an encyclopedia.

Hippopotamus   Monkey   Elephant

Pig   Dog   Whale

11.

More than 1 ton	Less than 1 ton

Practice 3   Measuring Capacity

Find the capacity of each container.

1.   The pitcher can hold _____ cups of water.

2.   The pitcher has a capacity of _____ cups.

3.   The vase can hold _____ pints of water.

4.   The vase has a capacity of _____ pints.

5.   The carton can hold _____ cups of milk.

6.   The carton has a capacity of _____ cups.

Find the capacity of each container.

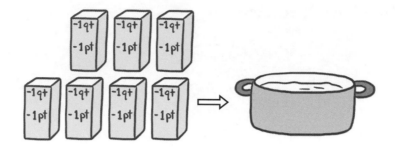

7. The pot can hold _____ quarts of soup.

8. The pot has a capacity of _____ quarts.

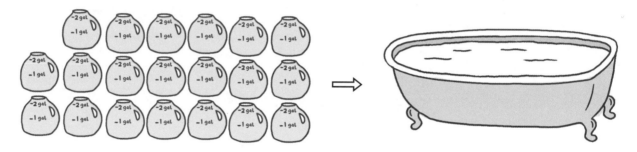

9. The bathtub can hold _____ gallons of water.

10. The bathtub has a capacity of _____ gallons.

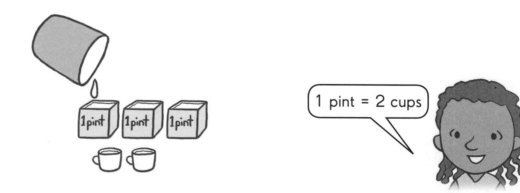

1 pint = 2 cups

11. This container can hold _____ cups of juice.

12. This container has a capacity of _____ cups.

Match.

13.

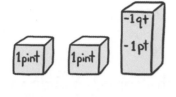   •   •

   •   •

   •   •

   •   •

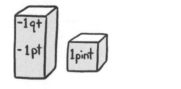   •   •

   •   •

Put On Your Thinking Cap!

Challenging Practice

Follow the directions to complete the drawing.

Step 1 Join the top of the lines at each end of the bus.

Step 2 Find the length of the bus in inches.

Step 3 Draw 3 ☐ square windows. Each has sides that are $\frac{1}{2}$ inch long.

Step 4 The windows are $\frac{1}{2}$ inch from the top of the bus.

Step 5 Draw a door between the two wheels. The height of the door is 1 inch. The width is $1\frac{1}{2}$ inches.

Step 6 Find the height from the top of the windows to the bottom of the bus to the nearest inch.

Step 7 Color and decorate your bus.

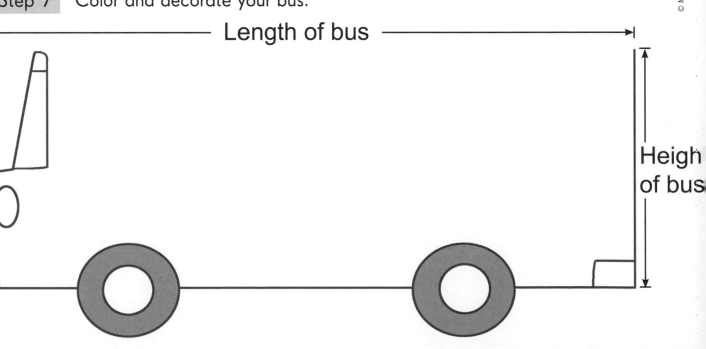

Length of bus

Height of bus

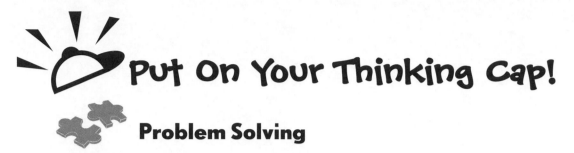

Put On Your Thinking Cap!

Problem Solving

The veterinarian at City Zoo keeps track of how much water each animal drinks in a period of time.
Decide which animal drinks the greatest amount of water and fill in the blank.

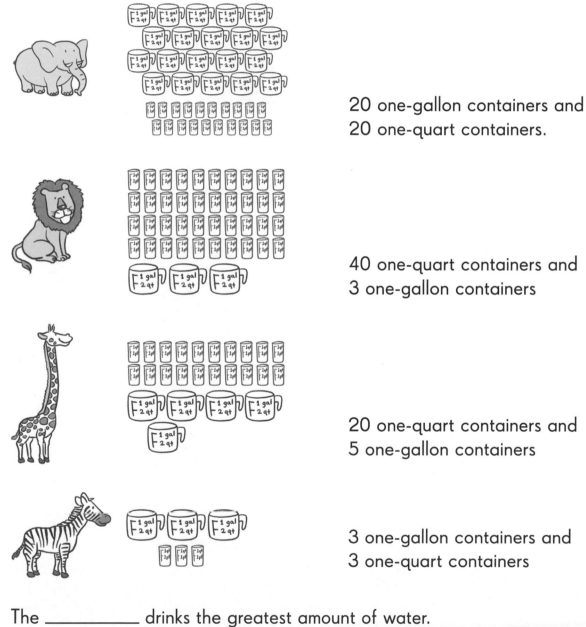

20 one-gallon containers and
20 one-quart containers.

40 one-quart containers and
3 one-gallon containers

20 one-quart containers and
5 one-gallon containers

3 one-gallon containers and
3 one-quart containers

The _____ drinks the greatest amount of water.

for Chapters 13 to 15

Concepts and Skills

Jessica is surveying and graphing her friends' favorite foods.

**Use the data in the tally chart to complete the bar graph.
Then answer the question.** *(Lesson 13.1)*

Kind of Food	Sandwich	Pizza	Salad	Pasta
Tally	⁙ l	⁙ ll ⁙	⁙ ⁙ ⁙	⁙ ⁙ ⁙ lll

1.

Favorite Food

Sandwich

Pizza

Kind of Food

Salad

Pasta

0   6   12   18   24

Number of Friends

2. How many friends did Jessica survey? _____

Complete. *(Lesson 14.1)*

3. The fraction shaded is _____.

4. The numerator of the fraction is _____.

5. The denominator of the fraction is _____.

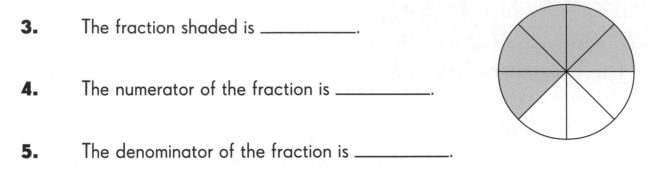

Write the missing numerator or denominator. *(Lesson 14.2)*

6. $\dfrac{3}{4} = \dfrac{\boxed{}}{12}$

7. $\dfrac{6}{8} = \dfrac{3}{\boxed{}}$

8. $\dfrac{\boxed{}}{5} = \dfrac{2}{\boxed{}} = \dfrac{\boxed{}}{20}$ *(Lesson 14.3)*

9. $\dfrac{8}{4} = \dfrac{6}{\boxed{}} = \boxed{}$ *(Lesson 14.3)*

Complete.
Express each fraction in simplest form. *(Lesson 14.3)*

10. $\dfrac{6}{10} =$ _____

11. $\dfrac{8}{12} =$ _____

Circle the fraction that is greater. *(Lesson 14.4)*

12. $\dfrac{5}{6}$ or $\dfrac{2}{3}$

13. $\dfrac{2}{5}$ or $\dfrac{5}{8}$

Name: _____   **Date:** _____

Circle the fraction that is less. *(Lesson 14.4)*

14. $\dfrac{5}{7}$ or $\dfrac{5}{9}$

15. $\dfrac{4}{9}$ or $\dfrac{5}{7}$

Compare. Write > or <. *(Lesson 14.4)*

16. $\dfrac{4}{5}$ $\bigcirc$ $\dfrac{3}{8}$

17. $\dfrac{3}{7}$ $\bigcirc$ $\dfrac{7}{12}$

Order the fractions from least to greatest. *(Lesson 14.4)*

18. $\dfrac{1}{2}$, $\dfrac{3}{8}$, $\dfrac{7}{12}$ _____

Order the fractions from greatest to least.

19. $\dfrac{1}{6}$, $\dfrac{3}{4}$, $\dfrac{2}{3}$ _____

Complete. Show each fraction on the number line. *(Lesson 14.4)*

$$\frac{1}{3}$$

$$0 \qquad \frac{1}{4} \qquad \frac{1}{2} \qquad \frac{3}{4} \qquad 1$$

> The example shows a fraction less than $\frac{1}{2}$ but greater than $\frac{1}{4}$.

20.   A fraction greater than $\dfrac{1}{2}$ but less than $\dfrac{3}{4}$ _____

21.   A fraction less than $\dfrac{1}{6}$ _____

22.   A fraction greater than $\dfrac{5}{6}$ _____

Color the pictures to find the fractional part of each set. *(Lesson 14.5)*

23. $\dfrac{1}{2}$ of 10

24. $\dfrac{3}{8}$ of 16

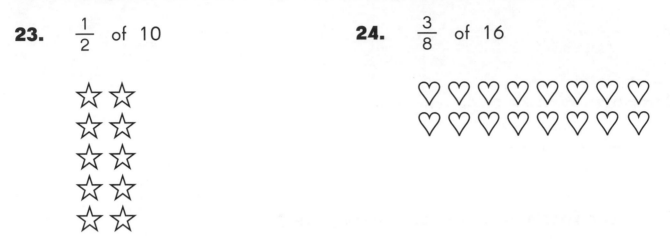

Write a fraction for the part of each set that is shaded. *(Lesson 14.6)*

25.

26.

_____   _____

Write two fractions to show the following whole numbers. *(Lesson 14.5)*

27. $2 = \dfrac{\Box}{\Box} = \dfrac{\Box}{\Box}$

28. $5 = \dfrac{\Box}{\Box} = \dfrac{\Box}{\Box}$

Complete. *(Lesson 14.5)*

29. $1 = \dfrac{4}{\Box}$

30. $2 = \dfrac{\Box}{8}$

Complete.
Measure Line segment A to the nearest: *(Lesson 15.1)*

31. inch. _____ in.

32. half inch. _____ in.

|←————————————→|
Line segment A

Measure the length of the rope to the nearest quarter inch. *(Lesson 15.1)*

33.

The length of the rope is _____ inches.

Measure the length of the pencil to the nearest quarter inch. *(Lesson 15.1)*

34.

The length of the pencil is _____ inches.

Choose the best unit of measure for measuring each length.
Write *inch, foot, yard,* or *mile.* *(Lesson 15.1)*

35. The width of a finger   _____

36. The length of a baseball bat   _____

37. The length of a playground   _____

38. The distance walked in 1 hour _____

Complete. *(Lesson 15.2)*

39.

The cherries weigh _____ ounces.

40.

Each loaf of bread weighs about 1 pound.

The pineapple weighs about _____ pounds.

Choose the best unit of measure for weighing each item. Write *ounce*, *pound*, or *ton*. *(Lesson 15.2)*

41. A dog _____

42. A box of toothpicks _____

43. A hippopotamus _____

Compare. Write > or <. *(Lesson 15.2)*

44. 1 oz ◯ 8 lb   **45.** 100 lb ◯ 100 ton

Complete. *(Lesson 15.3)*

46. The pitcher is completely filled with water.
The water is emptied into cups.

The capacity of the pitcher is about _____ cups.

47. 5 pints of water are poured to fill a container.

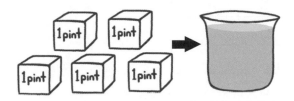

The capacity of the container is about _____ pints.

Circle the better estimate. *(Lesson 15.3)*

48. The capacity of a car's fuel tank is 20 gallons / 20 pints.

49. The amount of yogurt eaten for lunch is 1 cup / 1 quart.

Order from greatest capacity to least capacity. *(Lesson 15.3)*

50. 6 pt 14 qt 2 gal

51. 1 gal 18 cups 10 pt

_____

_____

Problem Solving

Miguel conducted a survey to find the number of hours that some students spend playing their favorite sport each week.

He recorded the data in a table.

Hours Spent on Favorite Sport

Favorite Sport	Number of Hours
Gymnastics	4
Football	6
Swimming	8
Jogging	8
Tennis	6
Cross Country	7
Baseball	6
Softball	6
Biking	8
Lacrosse	6
Volleyball	7
Soccer	6

Show the data on a line plot.
Give your line plot a title.

52.

_____

Answer each question.
Use the data on your line plot.

53. How many students spend more than 5 hours on their

favorite sport? _____

54. How many hours did most students spend on their favorite sport?

_____ hours

55. The number of students who spent 6 hours on their favorite sport is

_____ times the number of students who spent 7 hours.

56. There are _____ fewer students who spent 5 hours on their favorite

sport than those who spent 8 hours.

57. If a total of 15 students were surveyed, how many students do **not**

spend any time on sports? _____

The bar graph shows the number of points scored by four basketball players.

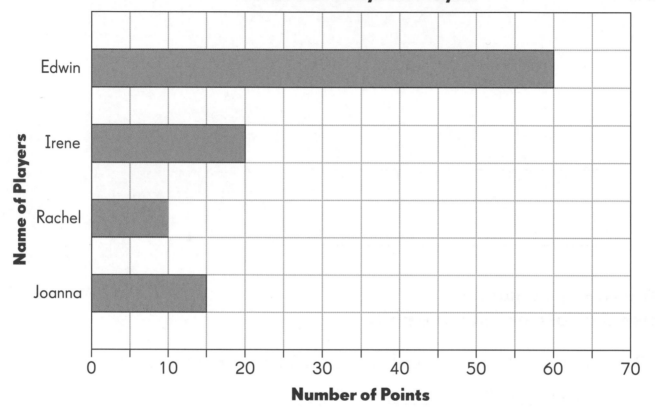

Points Scored by Four Players

Use the bar graph to answer the questions.

58. How many points did Edwin score? _____

59. Edwin scored 20 more points than Rachel.
How many points did Rachel score? _____

60. Use your answer from Exercise 59 to complete the bar graph for Rachel.

61. Edwin scored three times as many points as one of the players.

Who is this player? _____

62. Who scored the least number of points? _____

Chapter 16 Time and Temperature

Practice 1 Telling Time

Tell the time. Use *past*.

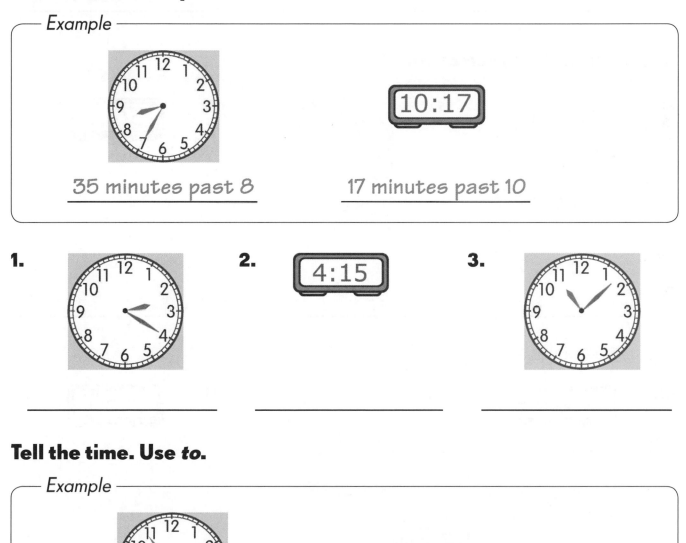

Example

35 minutes past 8

17 minutes past 10

1. _____

2. _____

3. _____

Tell the time. Use *to*.

Example

6 minutes to 3

32 minutes to 7

Tell the time. Use *to*.

4. _____

5. _____

6. _____

Tell the time. Use *past* or *to*.

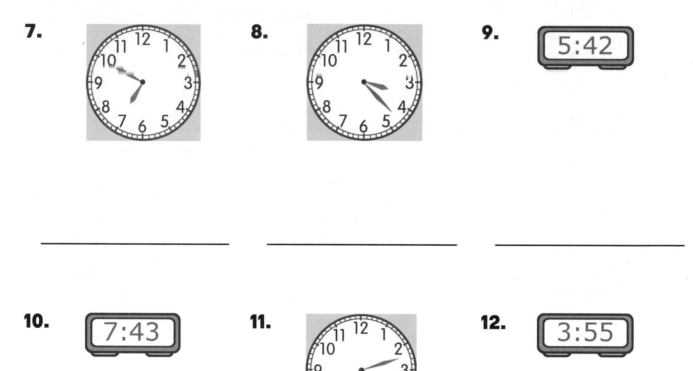

7. _____

8. _____

9. _____

10. _____

11. _____

12. _____

Tell the time in two ways.

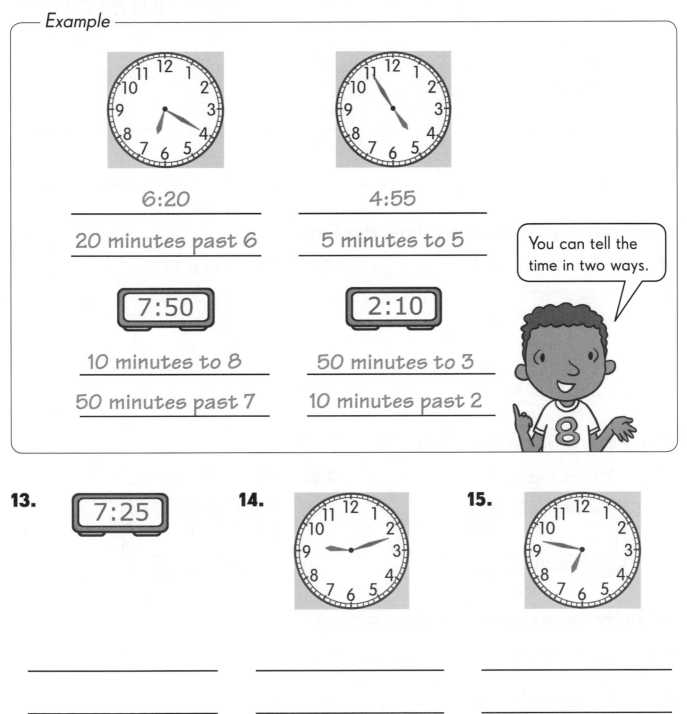

Example

6:20

20 minutes past 6

4:55

5 minutes to 5

7:50

10 minutes to 8

50 minutes past 7

2:10

50 minutes to 3

10 minutes past 2

You can tell the time in two ways.

13.   7:25

14.

15.

_____

_____

_____

_____

_____

_____

16.

17.

18.

_____

_____

_____

_____

_____

_____

Draw the minute hand to show the time.

19. 25 minutes past 11

20. 18 minutes to 7

Write the time on the clock.

21. 18 minutes to 1

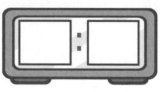

22. 25 minutes past 2

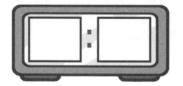

Fill in the blanks with the correct time.

23. 18 minutes past 2 is _____.

24. 15 minutes to 1 is _____.

25. 8:25 is _____ minutes past _____.

26. 6:50 is _____ minutes to _____.

Practice 2   Converting Hours and Minutes

Complete each number bond.

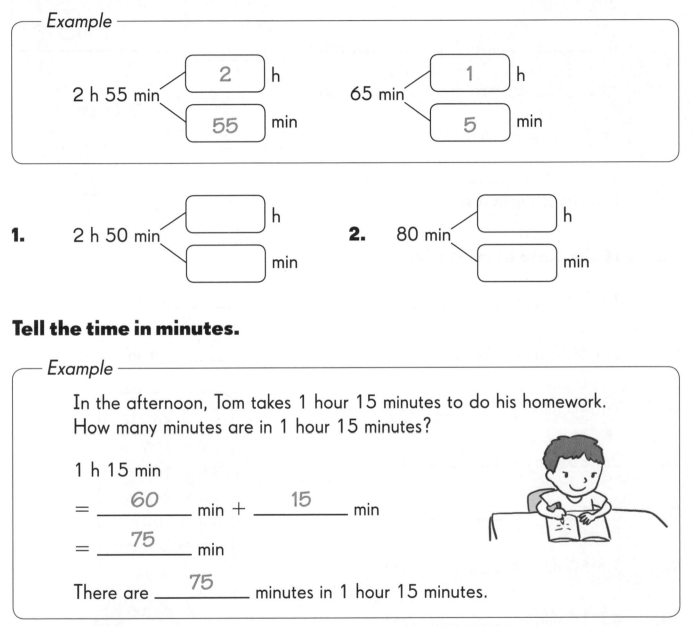

Example

2 h 55 min — [2] h / [55] min

65 min — [1] h / [5] min

1.   2 h 50 min — [ ] h / [ ] min

2.   80 min — [ ] h / [ ] min

Tell the time in minutes.

Example

In the afternoon, Tom takes 1 hour 15 minutes to do his homework.
How many minutes are in 1 hour 15 minutes?

1 h 15 min

= _____60_____ min + _____15_____ min

= _____75_____ min

There are _____75_____ minutes in 1 hour 15 minutes.

Tell the time in minutes.

3. Katie took 3 hours 20 minutes to sew two sets of curtains.
How many minutes are in 3 hours 20 minutes?

3 h 20 min

= _____ min + _____ min

+ _____ min + _____ min

= _____ min

There are _____ minutes in
3 hours 20 minutes.

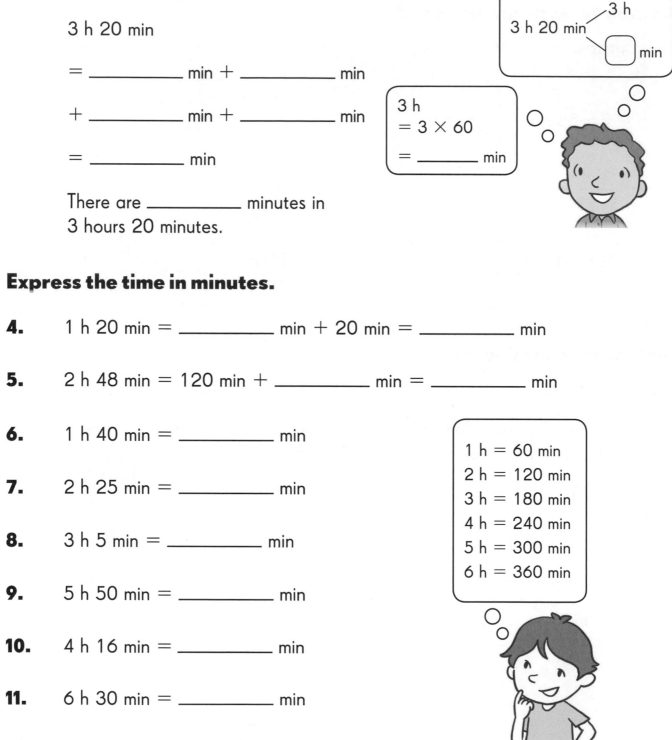

3 h 20 min $\diagup$ 3 h

$\bigsqcup$ min

3 h
= 3 × 60
= _____ min

Express the time in minutes.

4. 1 h 20 min = _____ min + 20 min = _____ min

5. 2 h 48 min = 120 min + _____ min = _____ min

6. 1 h 40 min = _____ min

7. 2 h 25 min = _____ min

8. 3 h 5 min = _____ min

9. 5 h 50 min = _____ min

10. 4 h 16 min = _____ min

11. 6 h 30 min = _____ min

1 h = 60 min
2 h = 120 min
3 h = 180 min
4 h = 240 min
5 h = 300 min
6 h = 360 min

Express the time in hours.

12.   180 min = _____ h

13.   360 min = _____ h

14.   120 min = _____ h

15.   240 min = _____ h

16.   480 min = _____ h

17.   300 min = _____ h

18.   420 min = _____ h

180 min
= 3 × 60 min
= 3 h

Express the time in hours and minutes.

19.   Sally took 70 minutes to do her homework.
How many hours and minutes are in 70 minutes?

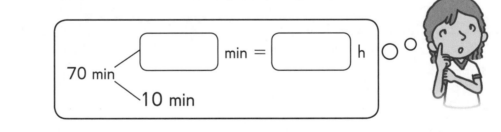

70 min ___ [   ] min = [   ] h

70 min = _____ min + _____ min

= _____ h _____ min

There are _____ hour _____ minutes in 70 minutes.

Express the time in hours and minutes.

20.   70 min = _____ h _____ min

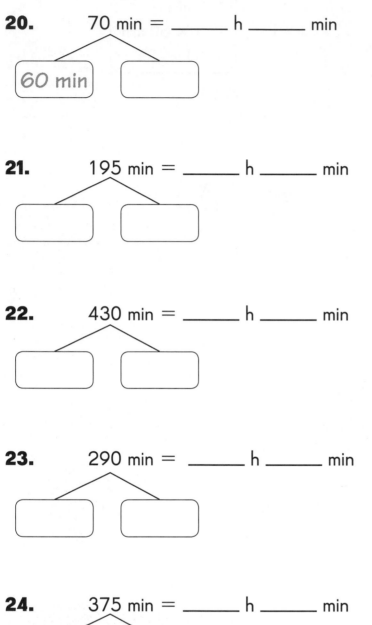

60 min

60 min = 1 h
70 − 60 = 10
So, 70 min = 1 h 10 min.

21.   195 min = _____ h _____ min

22.   430 min = _____ h _____ min

23.   290 min = _____ h _____ min

24.   375 min = _____ h _____ min

25.   255 min = _____ h _____ min

Practice 3 Adding Hours and Minutes

Step 1
Add the hours.
Step 2
Add the minutes.

Add.

Example

2 h 15 min + 2 h 20 min = ?

2 h   15 min   2 h   20 min

So, 2 h 15 min + 2 h 20 min

= __4__ h __35__ min.

__2__ h + __2__ h = __4__ h

__15__ min + __20__ min = __35__ min

__4__ h + __35__ min = __4__ h __35__ min

1. 3 h 25 min + 5 h 30 min = ?

3 h   25 min   5 h   30 min

So, 3 h 25 min + 5 h 30 min

= ___ h ___ min.

___ h + ___ h = ___ h

___ min + ___ min = ___ min

___ h + ___ min = ___ h ___ min

2. 7 h 30 min + 3 h 14 min = ?

7 h   30 min   3 h   14 min

So, 7 h 30 min + 3 h 14 min

= ___ h ___ min.

___ h + ___ h = ___ h

___ min + ___ min = ___ min

___ h + ___ min = ___ h ___ min

3. 2 h 50 min + 1 h 9 min = ?

2 h   50 min   1 h   9 min

So, 2 h 50 min + 1 h 9 min

= ___ h ___ min.

___ h + ___ h = ___ h

___ min + ___ min = ___ min

___ h + ___ min = ___ h ___ min

Add.

4. 20 min + 55 min = _____ min

_____ min = _____ h _____ min

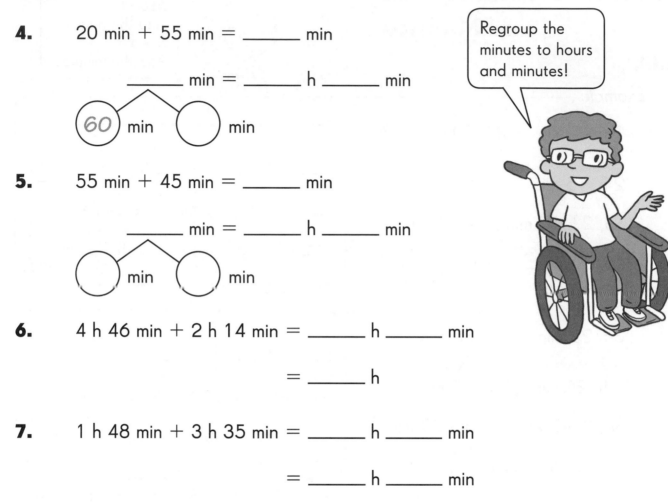

Regroup the minutes to hours and minutes!

5. 55 min + 45 min = _____ min

_____ min = _____ h _____ min

6. 4 h 46 min + 2 h 14 min = _____ h _____ min

= _____ h

7. 1 h 48 min + 3 h 35 min = _____ h _____ min

= _____ h _____ min

Solve.

8. Grace spends 50 minutes practicing the piano.
Then she spends 2 hours 15 minutes doing her homework.
How long does she spend on the two tasks?

Practice 4 Subtracting Hours and Minutes

Step 1
Subtract the hours.
Step 2
Subtract the minutes.

Subtract.

Example

7 h 20 min − 3 h 10 min = ?

7 h 20 min   3 h 10 min

So, 7 h 20 min − 3 h 10 min

= __4__ h __10__ min.

__7__ h − __3__ h = __4__ h

__20__ min − __10__ min = __10__ min

__4__ h + __10__ min = __4__ h __10__ min

---

1. 8 h 20 min − 7 h 15 min = ?

8 h 20 min   7 h 15 min

So, 8 h 20 min − 7 h 15 min

= ___ h ___ min.

___ h − ___ h = ___ h

___ min − ___ min = ___ min

___ h + ___ min = ___ h ___ min

---

2. 4 h 35 min − 1 h 15 min = ?

4 h 35 min   1 h 15 min

So, 4 h 35 min − 1 h 15 min

= ___ h ___ min.

___ h − ___ h = ___ h

___ min − ___ min = ___ min

___ h + ___ min = ___ h ___ min

---

3. 3 h 55 min − 2 h 30 min = ?

3 h 55 min   2 h 30 min

So, 3 h 55 min − 2 h 30 min

= ___ h ___ min.

___ h − ___ h = ___ h

___ min − ___ min = ___ min

___ h + ___ min = ___ h ___ min

Subtract.

4. 2 h 20 min − 1 h 50 min = _____ h _____ min

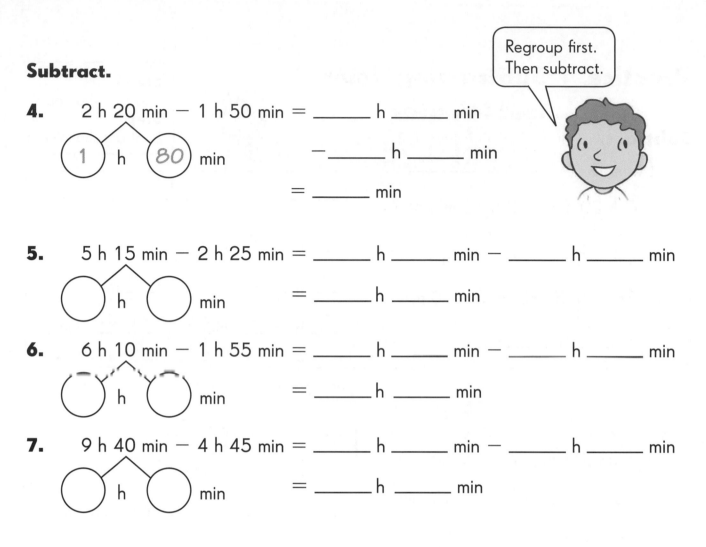

(1) h (80) min

     − _____ h _____ min

     = _____ min

Regroup first.
Then subtract.

5. 5 h 15 min − 2 h 25 min = _____ h _____ min − _____ h _____ min

    ◯ h ◯ min   = _____ h _____ min

6. 6 h 10 min − 1 h 55 min = _____ h _____ min − _____ h _____ min

    ◯ h ◯ min   = _____ h _____ min

7. 9 h 40 min − 4 h 45 min = _____ h _____ min − _____ h _____ min

    ◯ h ◯ min   = _____ h _____ min

Solve.

8. Rita takes 3 hours 5 minutes to sew a dress.
Tara takes 2 hours 40 minutes to sew a similar dress.
How much longer does Rita take to sew the dress than Tara?

Practice 5 Elapsed Time

Tell what time it will be.

1.　2 hours after 8:00 P.M. _____

2.　3 hours before 6:40 A.M. _____

3.　30 minutes after 1:36 P.M. _____

4.　45 minutes before 7:05 A.M. _____

5.　3 hours after 10:25 A.M. _____

6.　2 hours before 1:20 P.M. _____

Find the elapsed time. Draw a timeline to help you.

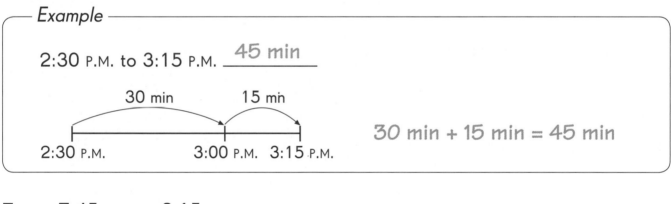

Example

2:30 P.M. to 3:15 P.M. _____45 min_____

30 min + 15 min = 45 min

7.　7:45 P.M. to 8:15 P.M. _____

8.　2:30 P.M. to 4:50 P.M. _____

Find the elapsed time. Draw a timeline to help you.

9. 7:45 A.M. to 9:50 A.M. _____

10. 11:30 P.M. to 2:10 A.M. _____

11. 11:25 A.M. to 3:10 P.M. _____

Write the correct time.
Draw the missing hands on each clock.

12.

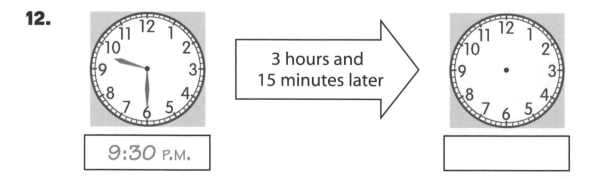

9:30 P.M.

3 hours and
15 minutes later

13.

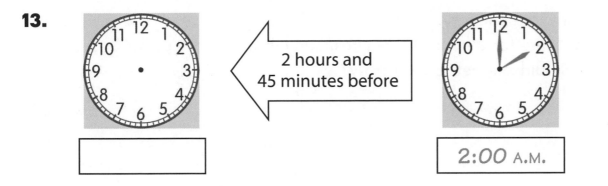

2 hours and
45 minutes before

2:00 A.M.

Solve.
Draw a timeline to help you.

14. Suki exercises every morning.
She starts at 6:30 A.M. and ends at 8:15 A.M.
How long does she exercise?

15. Devon started reading a book at 2:35 P.M.
She took 3 hours 10 minutes to finish the book.
What time did she finish reading the book?

16. Lissa went to the library.
She was there for 2 hours 15 minutes. She left the library at 5:40 P.M.
What time did she get to the library?

17. Marcus visited his friend's house from 11:50 A.M. to 3:15 P.M.
How long was his visit?

18. Mr. Nelson took 3 hours 30 minutes to decorate his classroom.
He started at 9:20 A.M.
What time did he finish?

19. Mrs. Martin's flight landed at 2:25 A.M.
The flight was 4 hours 45 minutes long.
What time did the flight take off?

Practice 6 Measuring Temperature

Fill in the blanks with these words.

1.

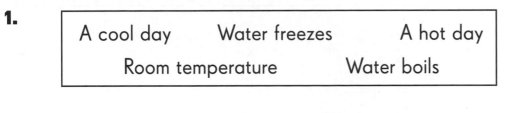

A cool day	Water freezes	A hot day
Room temperature		Water boils

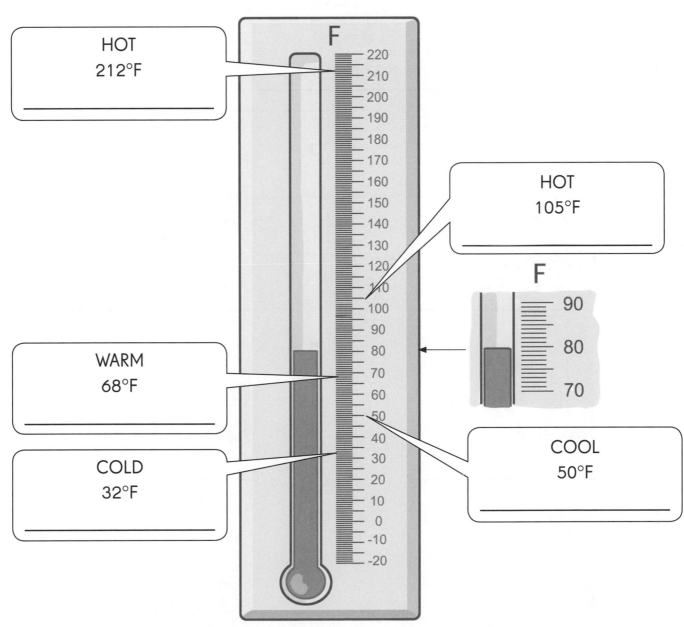

HOT
212°F

_____

HOT
105°F

_____

WARM
68°F

_____

COLD
32°F

_____

COOL
50°F

_____

Write each temperature using °F. Then write *hot*, *warm*, *cool*, or *cold* to describe the temperature.

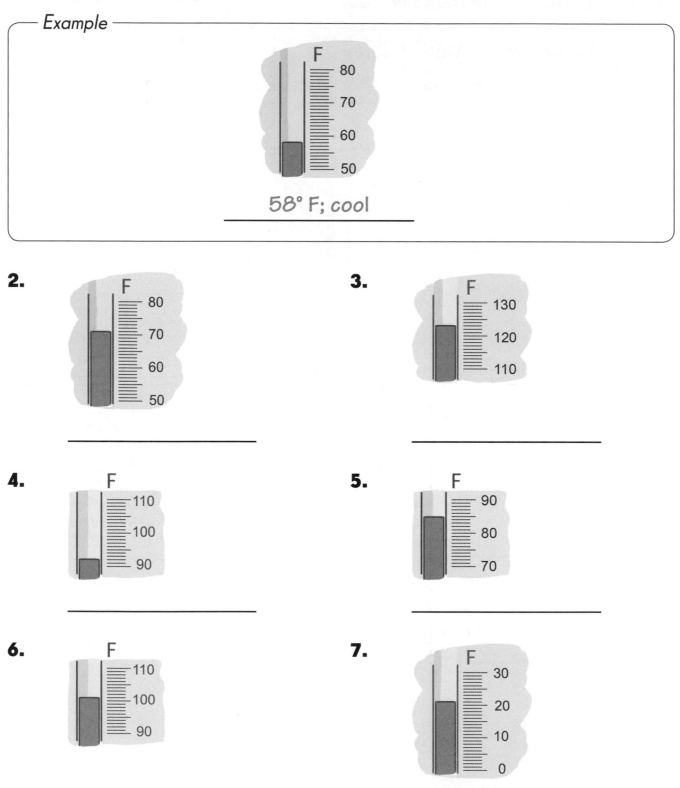

Example

58° F; cool

2. _____

3. _____

4. _____

5. _____

6. _____

7. _____

Circle the temperature that matches the activity.

8.

18°F   70°F

9.

98°F   102°F

Circle the picture that matches the temperature.

10.

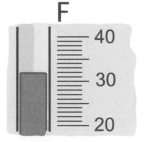

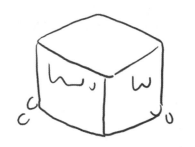

11.

Shade the temperature on each thermometer.

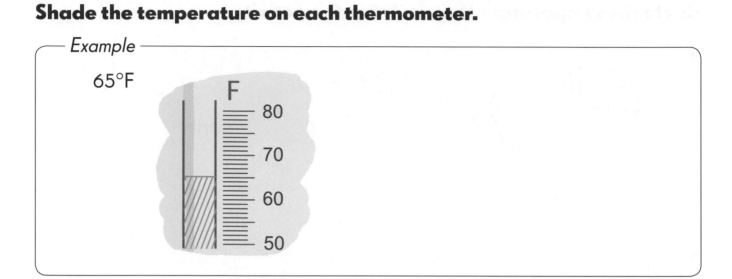

Example

65°F

---

12. 50°F

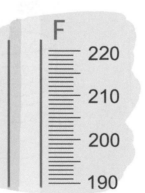

13. 32°F

14. 212°F

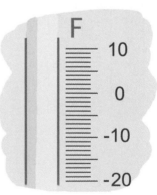

15. 0°F

Fill in the blanks.

16. Water boils at _____°F.

17. Water freezes at _____°F.

Practice 7 Real-World Problems: Time and Temperature

Solve.

1.   A watch is 15 minutes slow.
It shows 12:50 A.M.
What is the actual time?

Draw a timeline to help you solve the problem.

2.   A clock is 20 minutes fast.
It shows 9:35 P.M.
What is the actual time?

3. Joseph takes 50 minutes to install a software program.
How long does he take to install 4 such software programs?
Give your answer in hours and minutes.

4. Mr. Sperando left home at 6:35 A.M.
He took 1 hour 5 minutes to travel to his office.
What time did he reach his office?

5. Elaine spends 5 hours 30 minutes in school.
If she reaches school at 9:00 A.M.
What time does she leave school?

6. Heather has a dance lesson after school.
School ends at 2:55 P.M.
It takes Heather 15 minutes to walk to her dance studio.
After her 1 hour lesson, it takes Heather 15 minutes to walk home.
What time does Heather get home?

7. Derek takes 30 minutes to make one friendship bracelet.

    a. How many hours does he take to make 8 similar bracelets?

    b. How many similar bracelets can he make in 10 hours?

1 hour = 60 minutes
1 friendship bracelet → 30 minutes

8. Hannah left home at 6:15 A.M.

    She took 1 hour 55 minutes to ride to Maple Park and

    2 hours 20 minutes to ride home. She did not spend any time at the park.

    a. How long did she spend riding in all?

    b. What time did she return home?

9. Twyla sews teddy bears. She takes 3 hours 40 minutes to sew the
first teddy bear and 2 hours 55 minutes to sew the second teddy bear.
She finishes sewing the teddy bears at 8:10 P.M.
What time did she start sewing?

10. Jim finished work at 5:10 P.M. according to his watch.
His watch was 15 minutes slow.
a. What was the actual time he finished work?
b. He worked for 8 hours 15 minutes. What was the actual time
he started work?

Complete each story.
Use the temperatures and words in the box.

11.

70°F	212°F	12°F	cool
warm	hot	cold	

It was winter and the temperature outside was _____. It was

very _____ outside. Kate had set the heater to _____ and it

was _____ in the house. She put a kettle of water to boil and the

temperature of the water was _____. The water was _____

enough to make a hot drink.

12.

100°F	50°F
hot	cool

The temperature in the desert was a scorching _____. We drank water

to quench our thirst. The water was _____ because it was in a cooler.

Math Journal

- Example -

1. Here are the steps to do this subtraction exercise:

$$4 \text{ h } 30 \text{ min } - 2 \text{ h } 45 \text{ min}$$

Step 1   Regroup the 4 h to 3 h 60 min.

Step 2   Add 60 min to 30 min to get 90 min.

Step 3   Subtract 45 min from 90 min to get 45 min.

Step 4   Subtract 2 h from 3 h to get 1 h.

Step 5   Add 1 h and 45 min to get 1 h 45 min.

The steps to express time in hours and minutes are not in order.

Fill in the blanks.
320 min = _____ h _____ min

Order the steps by writing the step numbers in the boxes.

| Step | | 320 min is 5 h 20 min. |

| Step | | Subtract 300 min from 320 min to get 20 min. |

| Step | | Think 1 h = 60 min, 5 h = 300 min.
So, regroup 300 min to 5 h. |

2. David wanted to find out how much time Garrett took to make a kite.

Garrett started at 2:20 P.M. and ended at 5:05 P.M.

David drew this timeline to help him find how much time had passed:

```
    ┠─────────────────────────────┼──┨
 2:20 P.M.                   5:00 P.M.  5:05 P.M.
```

The timeline did not help him. Can you improve the time line so that it is easier for him to find how much time had passed?

```
    ┠─────────────────────────────┼──┨
 2:20 P.M.                   5:00 P.M.  5:05 P.M.
```

3. Imagine you and your friends are outdoors. The temperature is 90°F. Describe two activities you and your friends might want to do and the clothes that all of you should wear.

Explain your thinking.

_____

_____

_____

_____

_____

_____

Put On Your Thinking Cap!

Challenging Practice

Solve.

1.

Clock A   Clock B

Clock A is 25 minutes slow.
Clock B is 10 minutes fast.

a. What is the actual time? _____

b. What is the time shown on Clock B? _____

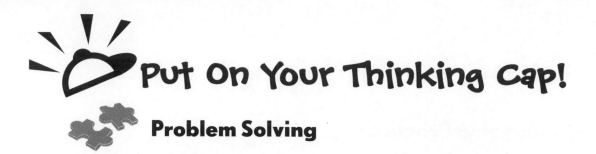

Put On Your Thinking Cap!

Problem Solving

Scientists in Snowland found that it is warmer in January than in July.
It is warmer in July than in June.
October is warmer than July but colder than January.
List these months in order from warmest to coldest.

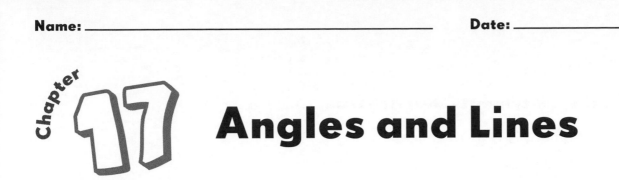

Angles and Lines

Practice 1 Understanding and Identifying Angles

Name each figure as a *point*, *line*, or *line segment*.

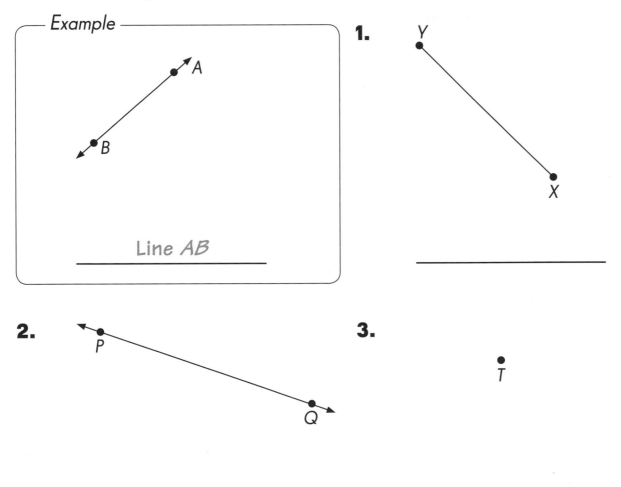

Example

A

B

Line AB

1. Y

X

_____

2. P

Q

_____

3.

T

_____

© Marshall Cavendish International (Singapore) Private Limited.

Check (✔) the statements that are true.

4. A line segment is part of a line. ☐

5. A point is an exact location in space. ☐

6. A line has two endpoints. ☐

Check (✔) the box if an angle is shown.

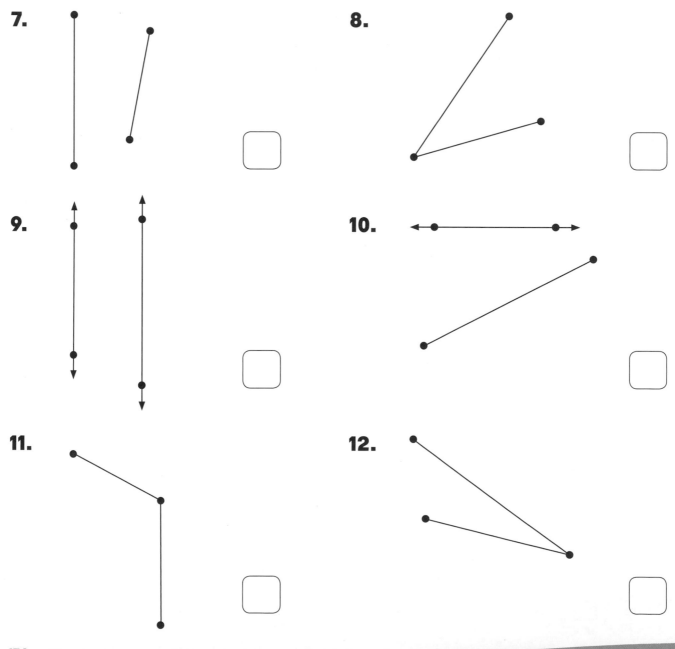

7. ☐

8. ☐

9. ☐

10. ☐

11. ☐

12. ☐

Mark two angles on each object.

13.

14.

15.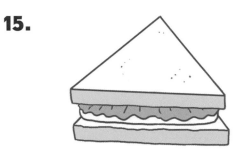

16.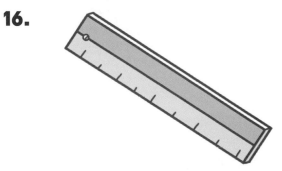

17.

18.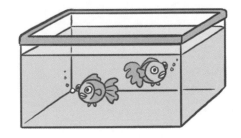

Mark two angles in each plane shape if possible.

19.

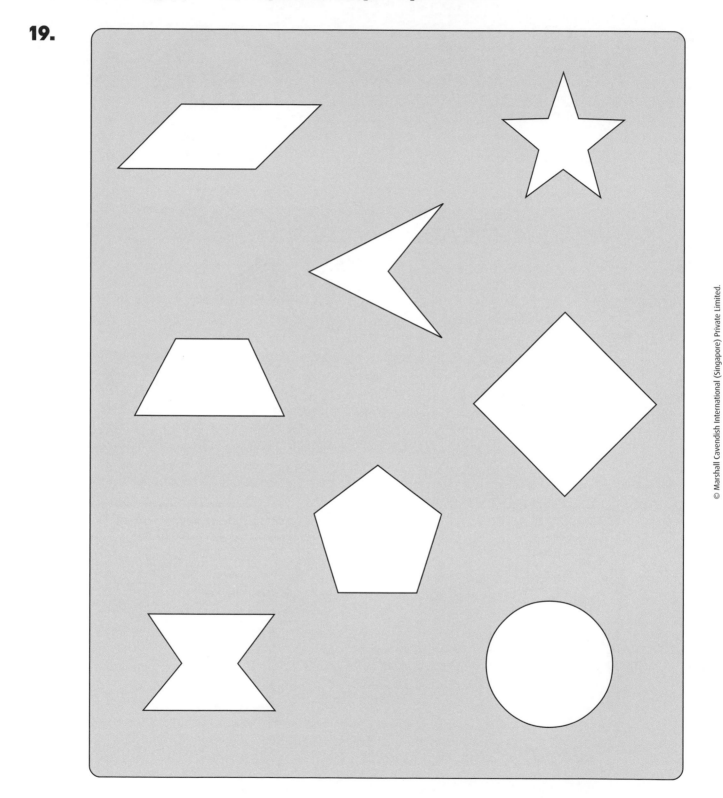

Complete the table.
Mark all the angles in each plane shape.

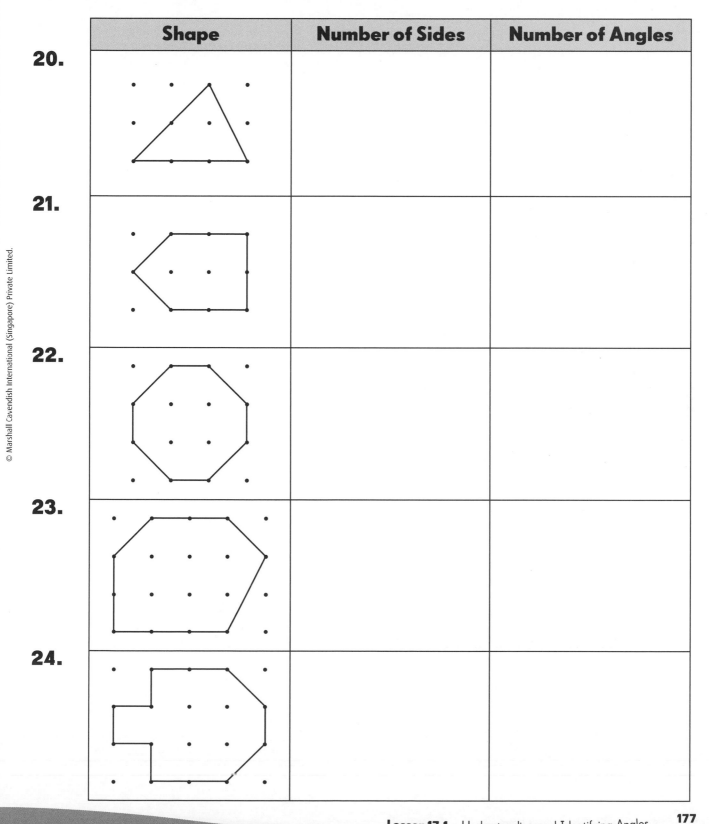

	Shape	Number of Sides	Number of Angles
20.			
21.			
22.			
23.			
24.			

Draw four different plane shapes.
Write the number of sides and angles in each shape.

25.

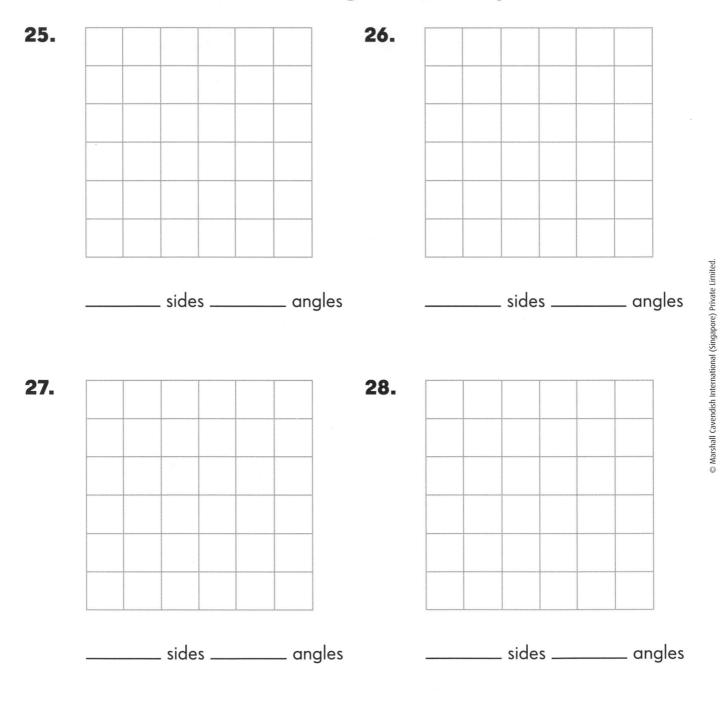

_____ sides _____ angles

26.

_____ sides _____ angles

27.

_____ sides _____ angles

28.

_____ sides _____ angles

Practice 2 Right Angles

Look at these angles.
Use a piece of folded paper   **to help you answer the questions.**

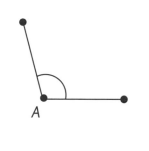

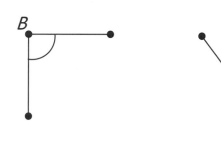

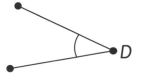

1.   Which angles are less than right angles?

Angles _____

2.   Which angle is greater than a right angle?

Angle _____

3.   Which angles are the same size as right angles?

Angles _____

Mark all the right angles in each figure.

4.

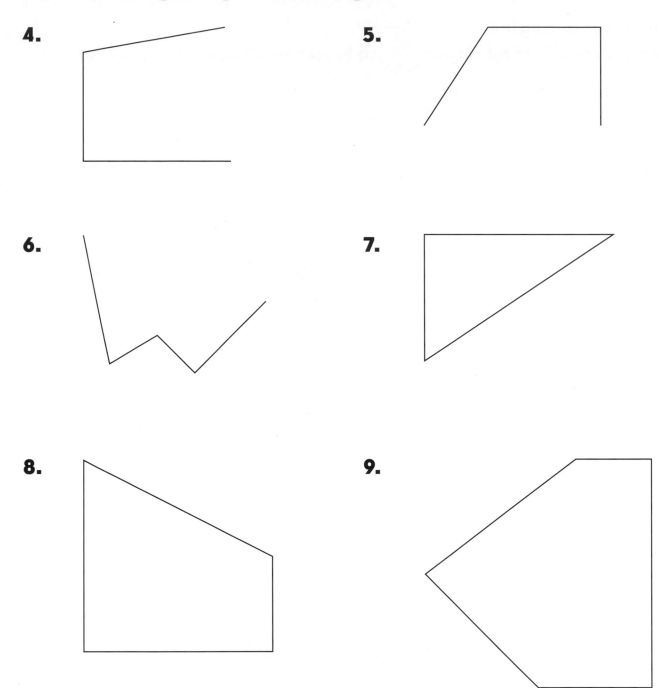

5.

6.

7.

8.

9.

Practice 3 Perpendicular Lines

Guess if the lines are perpendicular.
Use a ruler to check your guess.

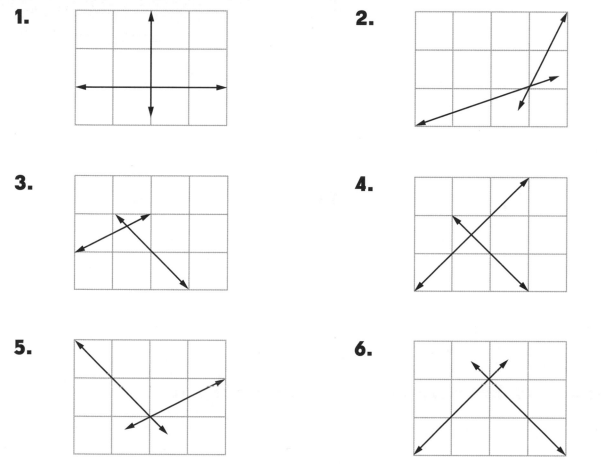

1.

2.

3.

4.

5.

6.

Check (✔) the box if the lines are perpendicular.

	1	2	3	4	5	6
Check (✔)						

Use a ruler to check for perpendicular lines.
Use a colored pencil to trace a pair of perpendicular lines
in each figure.

7.

8.

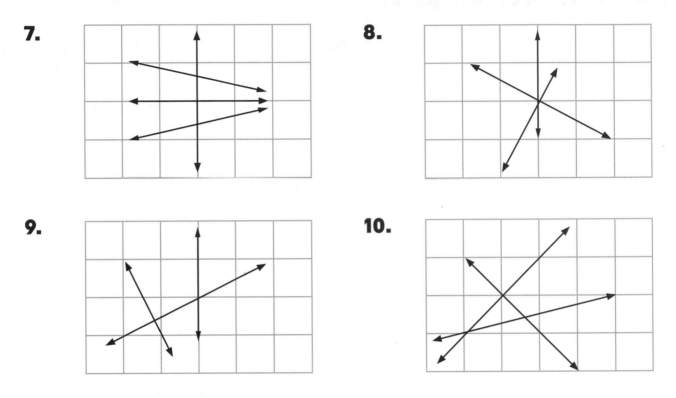

9.

10.

Circle the letters that have perpendicular line segments.

11.

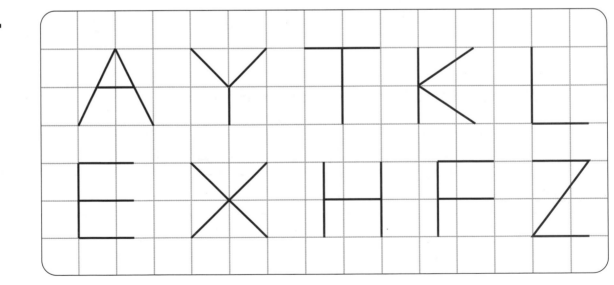

Name all the pairs of perpendicular line segments in each figure.

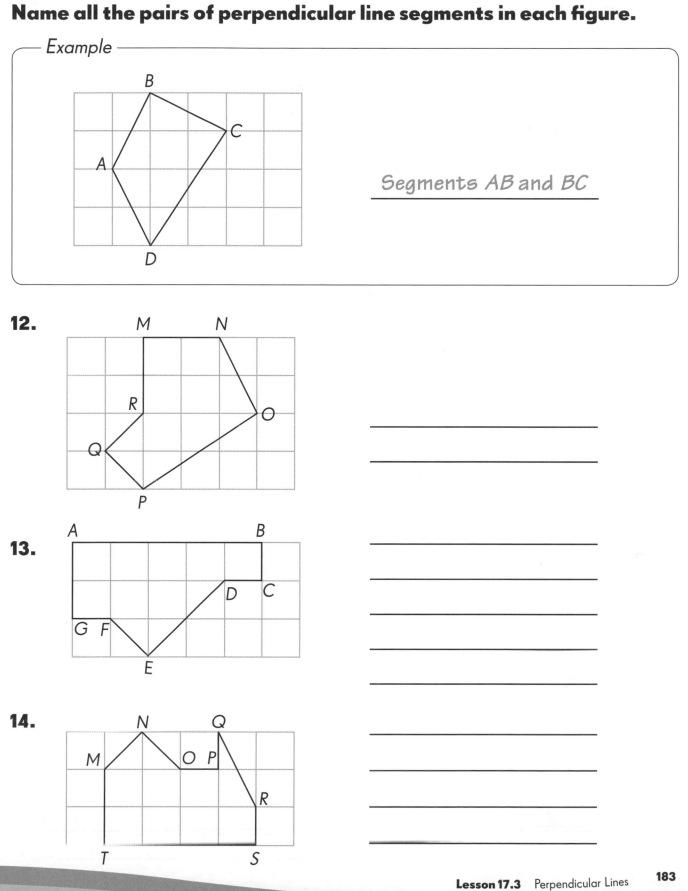

Example

Segments AB and BC
_____

12.

_____

_____

13.

_____

_____

_____

_____

_____

14.

_____

_____

_____

_____

Identify and name a pair of perpendicular line segments on each object.

15.

_____

16.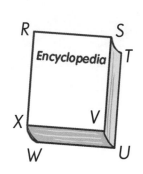

_____

Carry out this activity.

17. Think of two objects that have perpendicular line segments. Use the Internet to find pictures of these objects. Print and paste them below.
Use a colored pencil to trace a pair of perpendicular line segments on each object.

You can also look for the pictures in newspapers or magazines.

Practice 4 Parallel Lines

Guess if the lines are parallel.
Count square units between the lines to check your guess.

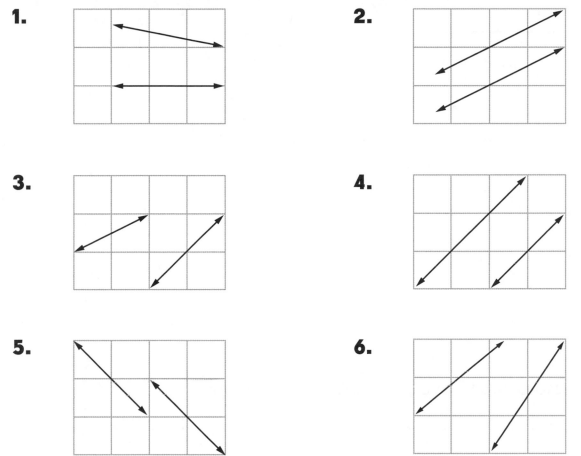

1.

2.

3.

4.

5.

6.

Check (✔) the box if the lines are parallel.

	1	2	3	4	5	6
Check (✔)						

Count square units between lines to find parallel lines. Use a colored pencil to trace a pair of parallel lines in each figure.

7.

8.

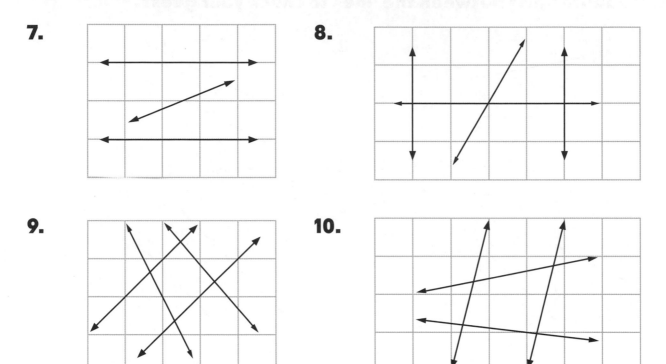

9.

10.

Circle the letters that have parallel line segments.

11.

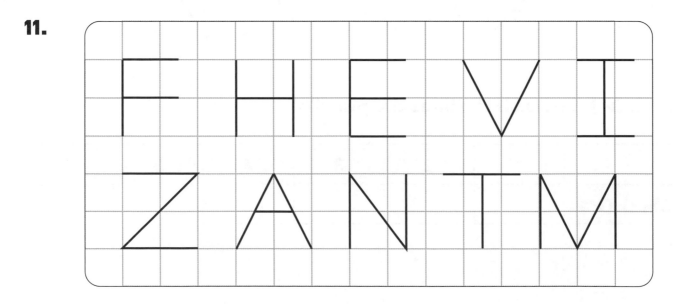

Name all the pairs of parallel line segments in each figure.

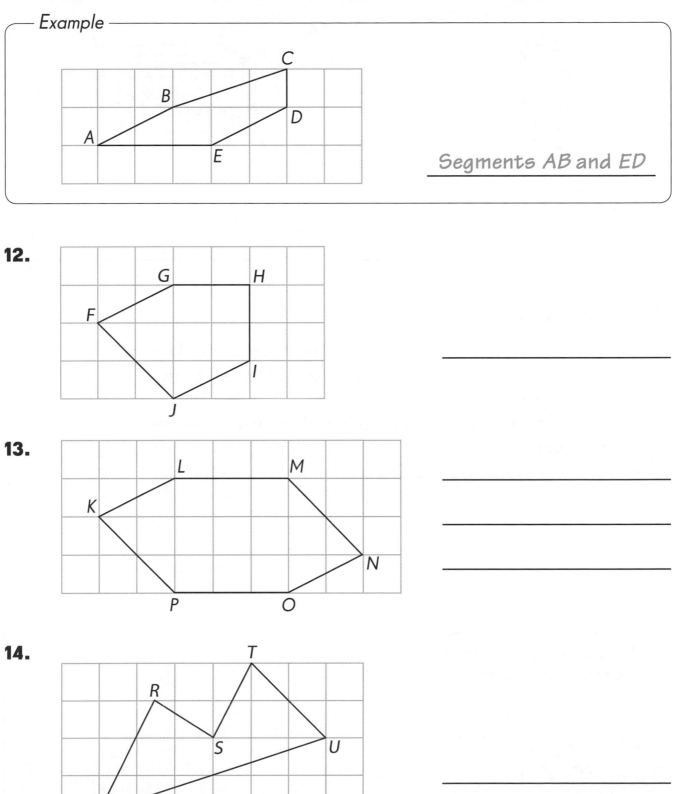

Example

Segments AB and ED

12. _____

13. _____

_____

_____

14. _____

Identify and name a pair of parallel line segments on each object.

15.

_____

16.

_____

Carry out this activity.

17. Think of two objects that have parallel line segments. Use the Internet to find pictures of these objects. Print and paste them below.
Use a colored pencil to trace a pair of parallel line segments on each object.

You can also look for the pictures in newspapers or magazines.

Math Journal

1. How would you explain perpendicular lines to a second grader?

_____

_____

2. How would you explain parallel lines to a younger brother or sister?

_____

_____

3. Lines that meet are perpendicular. Is this statement true?
Use figures to explain your answer.

4. Study the figure.

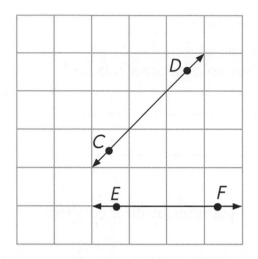

Line segment *CD* is not perpendicular to line segment *EF*.
How would you show that they are not parallel?

_____

_____

Put On Your Thinking Cap!

Challenging Practice

Draw each shape on the dot grid paper.

1.   A shape with 5 sides and
5 angles

2.   A shape with 3 sides and 2 angles
less than a right angle

3.   A shape with 4 sides and an
angle greater than a right angle

4.   A shape with 7 sides and 7 angles,
3 of which are right angles

Answer the questions.

5. Name two pairs of perpendicular line segments.

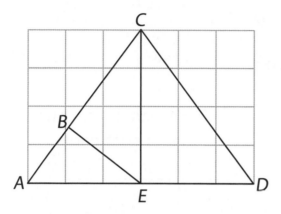

_____

_____

6. Name four line segments parallel to segment _NM_.

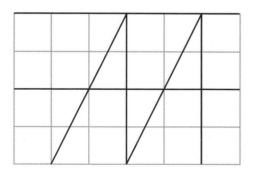

_____

_____

_____

_____

7. How many pairs of parallel line segments are in the diagram?

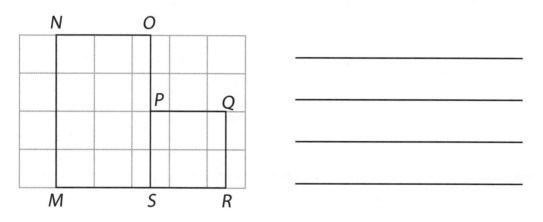

There are _____ pairs of parallel line segments.

Put On Your Thinking Cap!

Problem Solving

Draw shapes on dot grid paper. Then answer the questions.

1. Draw a triangle with a right angle.

Can you draw a triangle with 2 right angles? _____

2. Draw a shape with 4 sides and 2 right angles.

What do you notice about the other angles in the shape?

_____

Solve.

3. Five students are walking to school from their houses.
Look at the map.

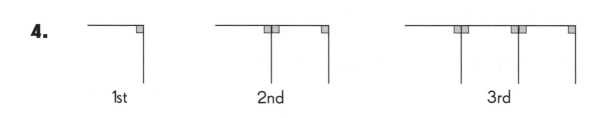

Which student's house is nearest to the school? Student _____
Draw a line segment to join this student's house to the school.
What do you notice about this line segment?

_____

4.

| 1st | 2nd | 3rd |

The pattern is made up of perpendicular line segments.
The 1st pattern has 1 right angle.
The 2nd pattern has 3 right angles.
The 3rd pattern has 5 right angles.
How many right angles will the 10th pattern have?

_____

Chapter 18 Two-Dimensional Shapes

Practice 1 Classifying Polygons

Circle the polygons.

1.

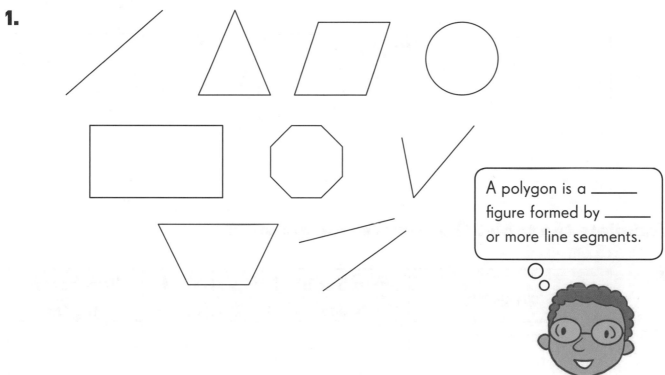

A polygon is a _____ figure formed by _____ or more line segments.

Mark the angles. Label the parts of each polygon.

2.

3.

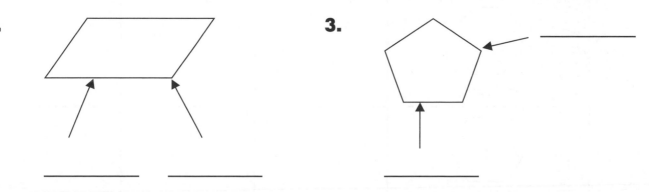

Identify each polygon.

4.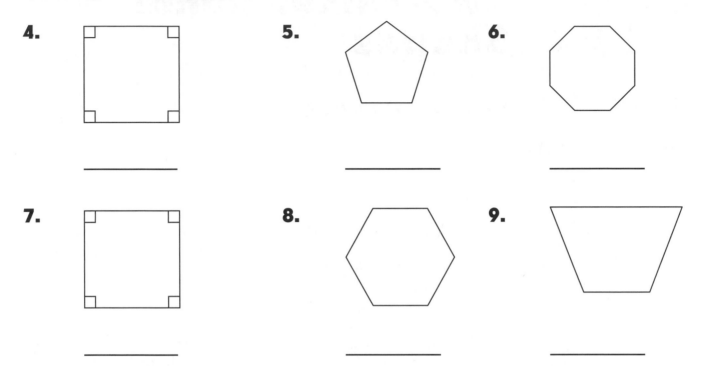

_____

5.

_____

6.

_____

7.

_____

8.

_____

9.

_____

Complete the table. Then answer the question.

10.

Polygons	Number of Sides	Number of Vertices	Number of Angles
square			
octagon			
hexagon			

Polygons	Number of Sides	Number of Vertices	Number of Angles
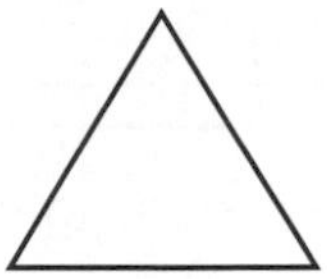 triangle			
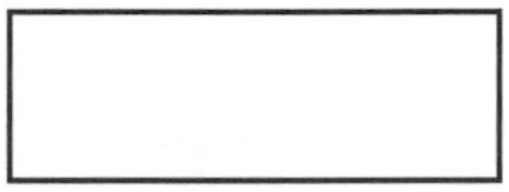 rectangle			
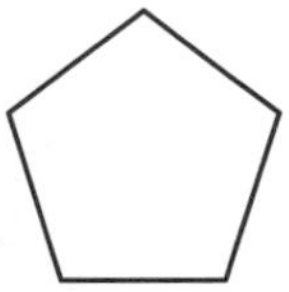 pentagon			
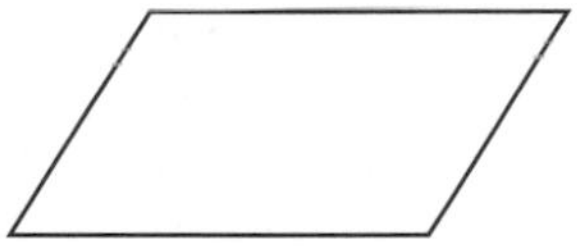 parallelogram			
 rhombus			
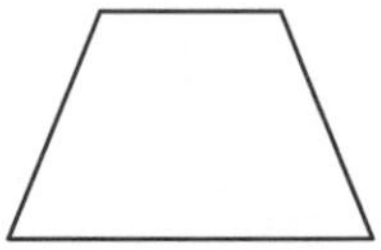 trapezoid			

11. Which figures have the same number of sides, vertices and angles?

_____

_____

> A square, rectangle, parallelogram, rhombus and trapezoid are some special polygons. They have _____ sides, vertices and angles.

Are these statements correct? Write *true* or *false*.

12. A hexagon has seven sides and six angles. _____

13. All polygons have four sides. _____

14. All parallelograms, squares, and trapezoids have

four angles. _____

15. An octagon has eight vertices and seven sides. _____

16. A pentagon has six angles. _____

17. A triangle has two vertices. _____

18. A parallelogram can be separated into 4 triangles. _____

19. A rectangle has four right angles. _____

Cut out the tangram below and complete the table.

20.

Kind of Polygon	Number of Polygons

Use at least 5 polygons to make a figure. Complete the table.

21.

Kind of Polygon Used	Number of Polygons

22. Name the figure that you have made.

- ✂ - - - - - - - - - - - - - -

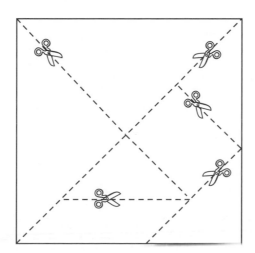

Solve.

23. I am a polygon. I have 1 more angle than

a rectangle has. What am I? _____

24. I am a polygon. I have 1 more side than

a pentagon has. What am I? _____

25. I am a polygon. I have 1 more vertex than

a triangle has. What am I? _____

26. Add one more polygon to the shape below to
make it a hexagon.

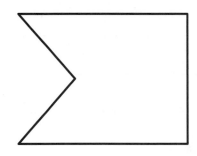

Identify each quadrilateral. Then explain your answer.

┌─ *Example* ───┐

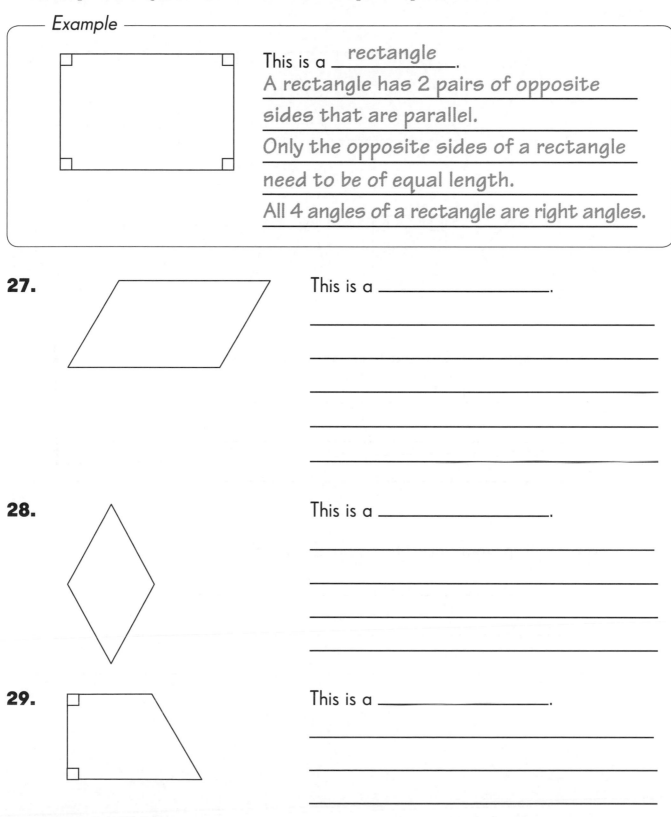

This is a ___rectangle___.

A rectangle has 2 pairs of opposite

sides that are parallel.

Only the opposite sides of a rectangle

need to be of equal length.

All 4 angles of a rectangle are right angles.

└──┘

27.

This is a _____.

_____

_____

_____

_____

_____

_____

28.

This is a _____.

_____

_____

_____

_____

_____

29.

This is a _____.

_____

_____

_____

_____

_____

_____

Write *P* for a parallelogram, *R* for rhombus, or *T* for trapezoid on the shapes.

30.

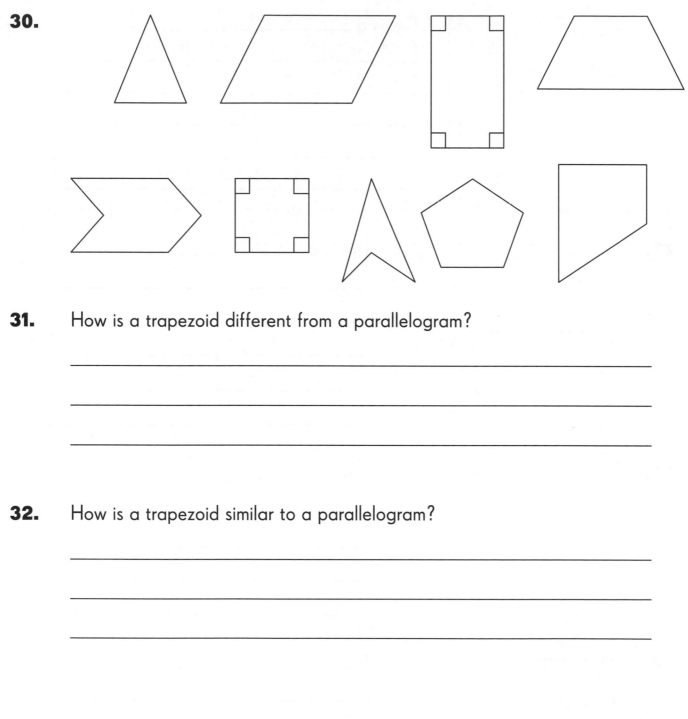

31. How is a trapezoid different from a parallelogram?

_____

_____

_____

32. How is a trapezoid similar to a parallelogram?

_____

_____

_____

Practice 2 Congruent Figures

Does Figure A show a flip of Figure B? Write *yes* or *no*.

1.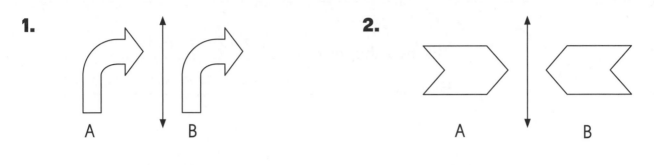

2.

_____   _____

Does Figure C show a slide of Figure D? Write *yes* or *no*.

3.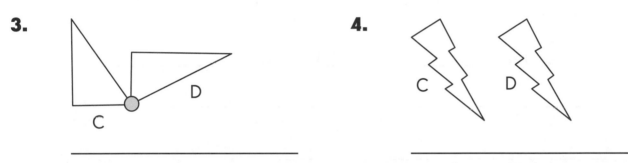

4.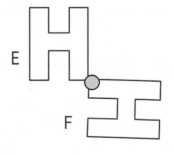

_____   _____

Does Figure E show a turn of Figure F? Write *yes* or *no*.

5.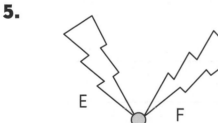

6.

_____   _____

Flips, slides, and turns are movements that change the position of figures but not their shape or size.

Look at the pairs of figures.
Identify and explain which pair is congruent and which is not.

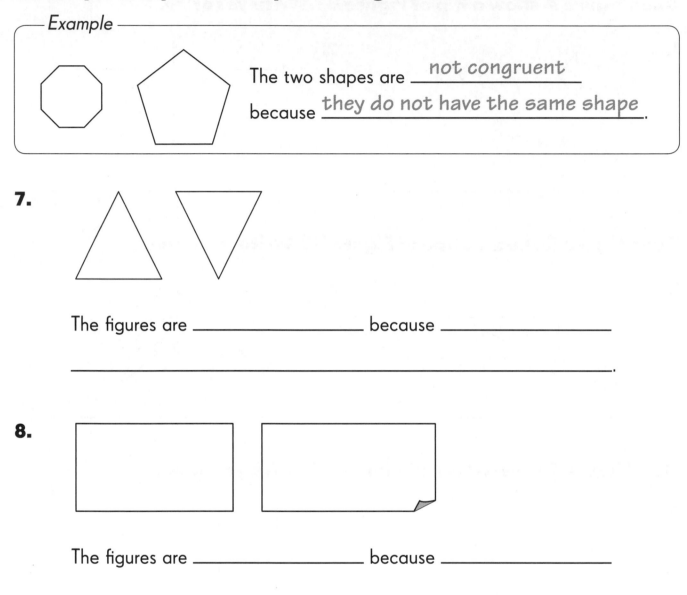

Example

The two shapes are ___not congruent___
because ___they do not have the same shape___.

7.

The figures are _____ because _____
_____.

8.

The figures are _____ because _____
_____.

Circle the pairs of congruent shapes.

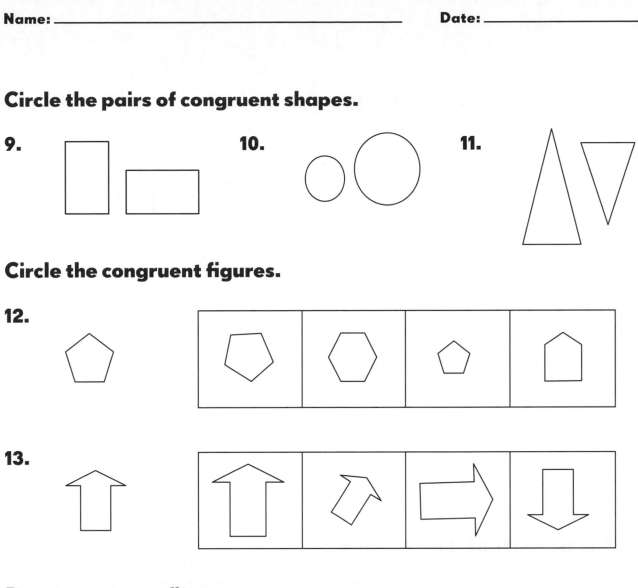

9.

10.

11.

Circle the congruent figures.

12.

13.

Draw congruent figures.
Trace the shape. Cut it out and draw a congruent figure by sliding it from left to right.

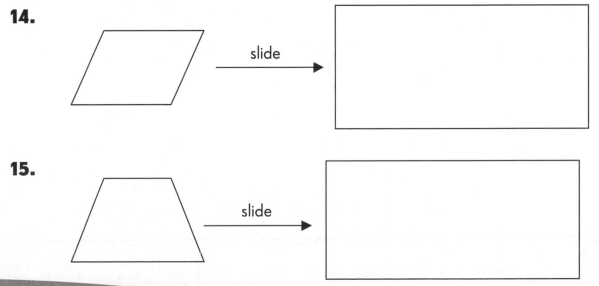

14.

slide

15.

slide

Circle the figure that shows a flip.

16.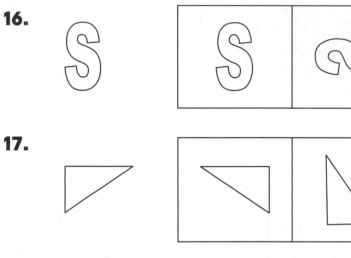

17.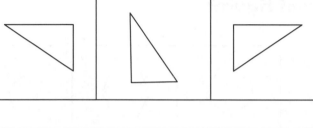

18.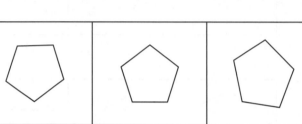

Circle the figure that shows a turn.

19.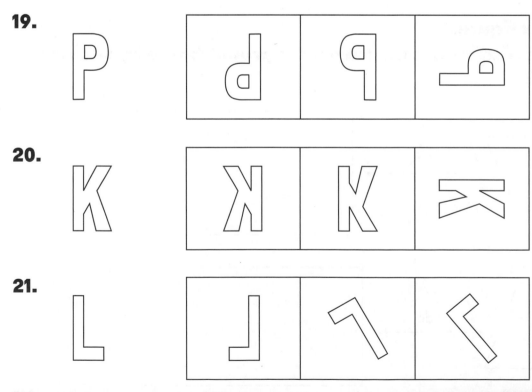

20.

21.

Practice 3 Symmetry

Circle the symmetric figures.

1.

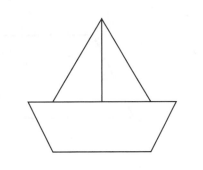

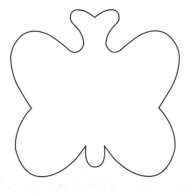

Decide which of the dotted lines are lines of symmetry.

2.

A figure has a line of symmetry when congruent halves match exactly when folded along a line.

Decide whether the line is a line of symmetry. Write *yes* or *no*.

3.

4.

5.

6.

7.

8.

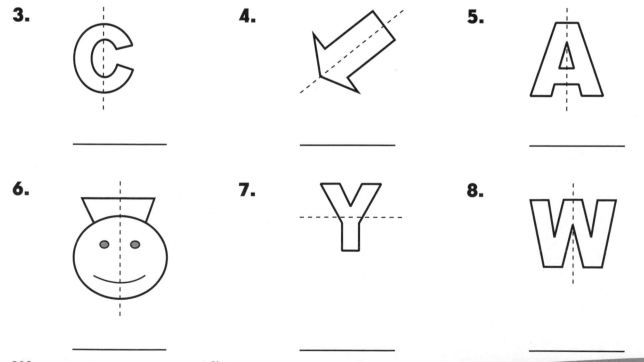

Put On Your Thinking Cap!

Challenging Practice

1. Copy the figure on a dot paper. Cut it out and rearrange the shapes in the figure to form a square.

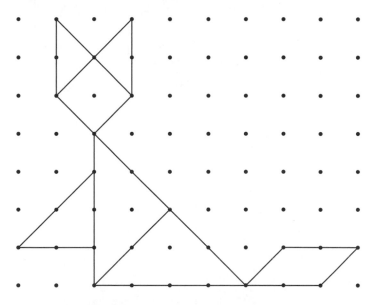

2. Study the pattern to find the rule.
Then draw the missing shape.

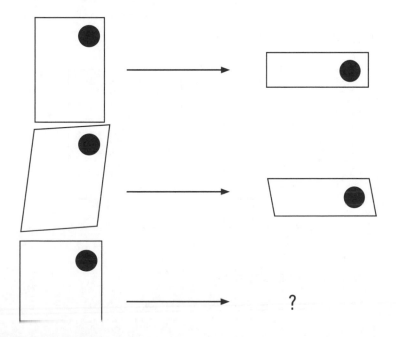

Put On Your Thinking Cap!

Problem Solving

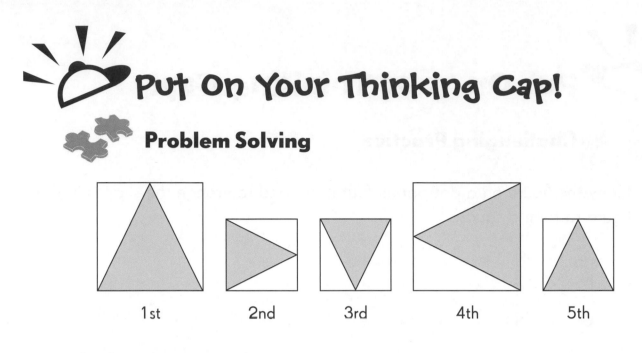

1st   2nd   3rd   4th   5th

1. Look at the repeated pattern.

  a. Check the box that shows the next shape.

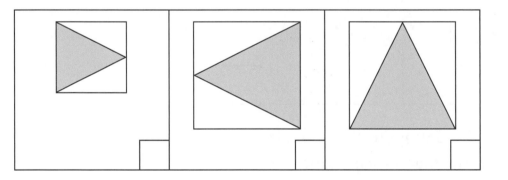

  b. Check the box that shows the tenth shape.

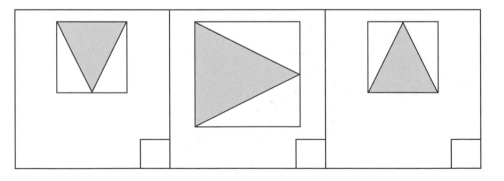

2. Describe the movement shown by the shapes.

Chapter 19
Area and Perimeter

Practice 1   Area

Draw and color two different figures. Use 4 squares (▢) and 2 half-squares (◺) for each figure.

1.

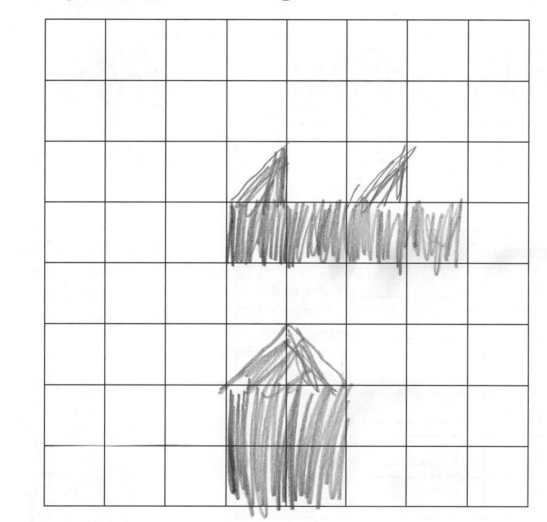

The figures are made of square and half-square tiles. Write the area of each figure in the table.

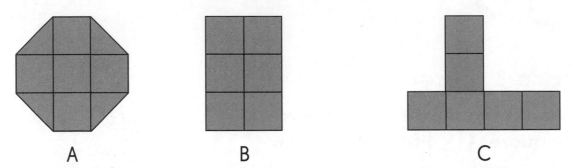

A   B   C

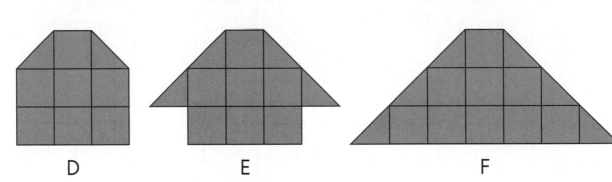

D   E   F

2.

Figure	Area
A	_____ square units
B	_____ square units
C	_____ square units
D	_____ square units
E	_____ square units
F	_____ square units

Each square (☐) is 1 square unit. Each half-square (◺) is $\frac{1}{2}$ square unit.

3. Figure _____ and Figure _____ have the same area.

4. Figure _____ has the largest area.

Draw two different figures with the same area on the grid.

5.

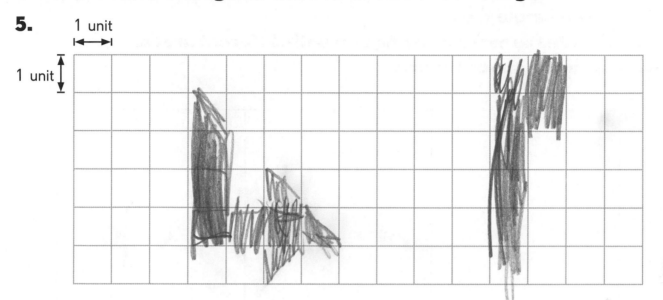

Add squares (☐) or half-squares (◺) to each figure to make its area 7 square units.

6.

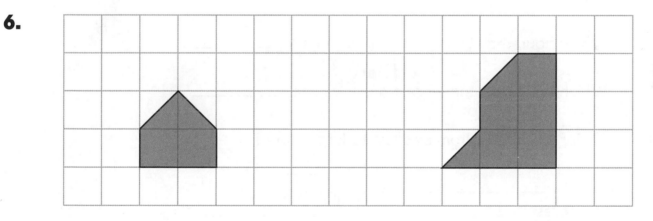

Complete.
Cut out the triangle tiles.
Use all the tiles to make three figures with different areas.
Glue them in the spaces below.

7.

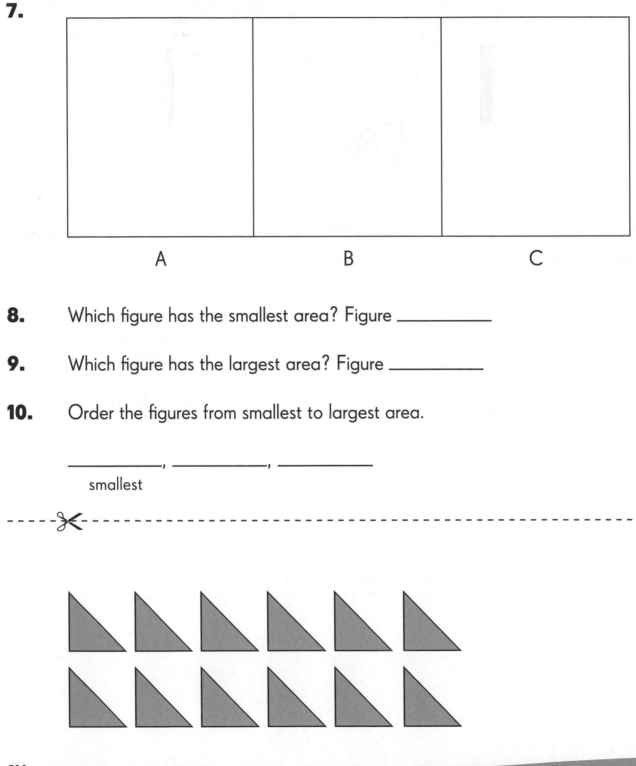

A   B   C

8. Which figure has the smallest area? Figure _____

9. Which figure has the largest area? Figure _____

10. Order the figures from smallest to largest area.

_____, _____, _____
smallest

Practice 2   Square Units (cm² and in.²)

**Find the area of each shaded figure in square centimeters (cm²).
Then complete the table.**

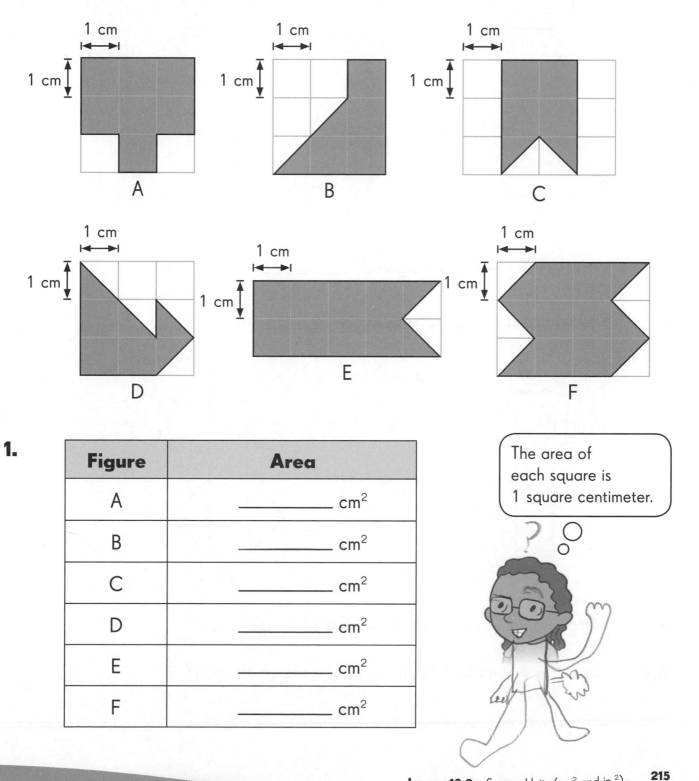

1.

Figure	Area
A	_____ cm²
B	_____ cm²
C	_____ cm²
D	_____ cm²
E	_____ cm²
F	_____ cm²

The area of
each square is
1 square centimeter.

Draw two different figures with the same area on the grids.

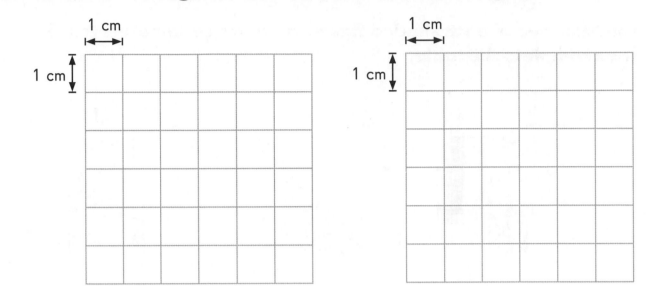

2. What is the area of the figures? _____

3. The figures are made of square and half-square tiles.
Find the area of each figure.

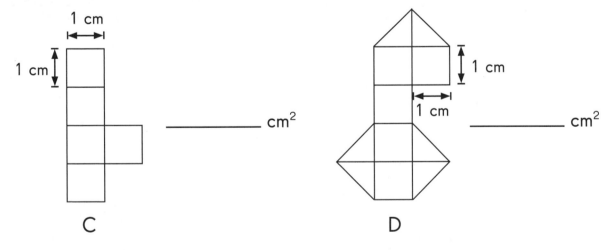

_____ cm²

C

_____ cm²

D

4. Which figure has a larger area? Figure _____

5. How can you make both figures have the same area?

_____

Name: _____ **Date:** _____

Find the area of each shaded figure in square inches.
Then complete the table.

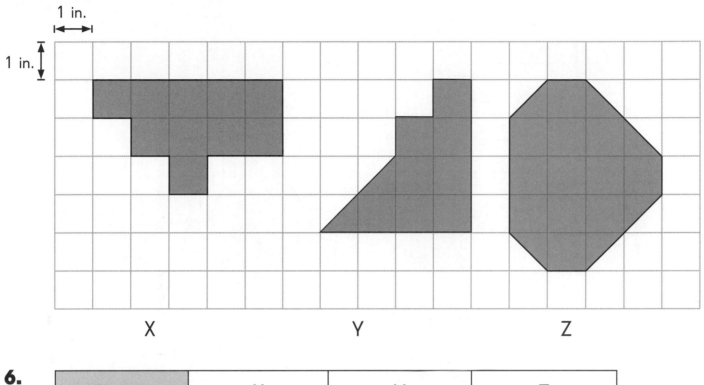

X   Y   Z

6.

Figure	X	Y	Z
Area	_____ in.²	_____ in.²	_____ in.²

Draw two different figures with the same area on the grid.

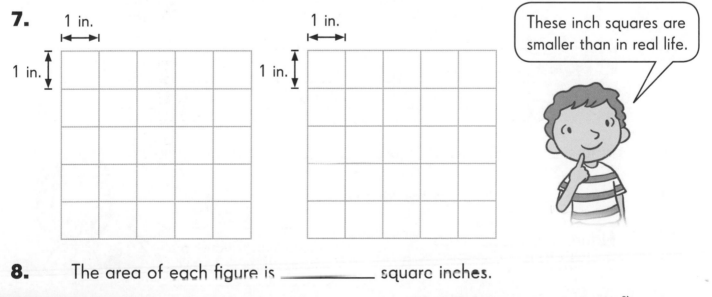

7.

1 in.   1 in.

These inch squares are smaller than in real life.

8. The area of each figure is _____ square inches.

Find the area of each shaded figure in square inches. Then complete the table.

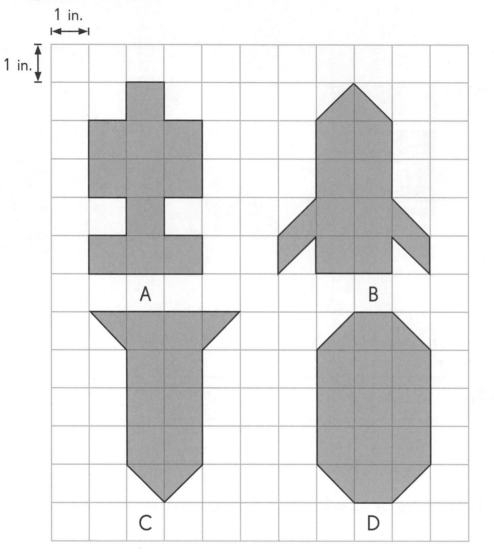

1 in.

1 in.

A

B

C

D

9.

Figure	A	B	C	D
Area	_____ in.²	_____ in.²	_____ in.²	_____ in.²

10. Figure _____ and Figure _____ have the same area.

11. Figure _____ has the largest area.

12. Figure _____ has the smallest area.

These inch squares are smaller than in real life.

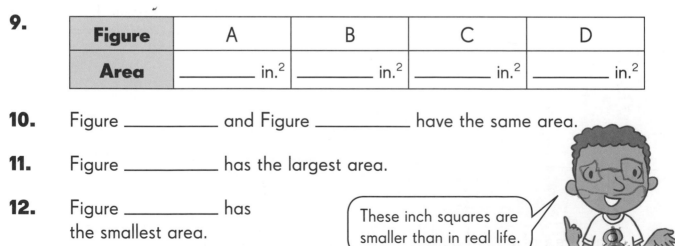

Practice 3 Square Units (m² and ft²)

Find the area of each shaded figure in square meters.
Then complete the table.

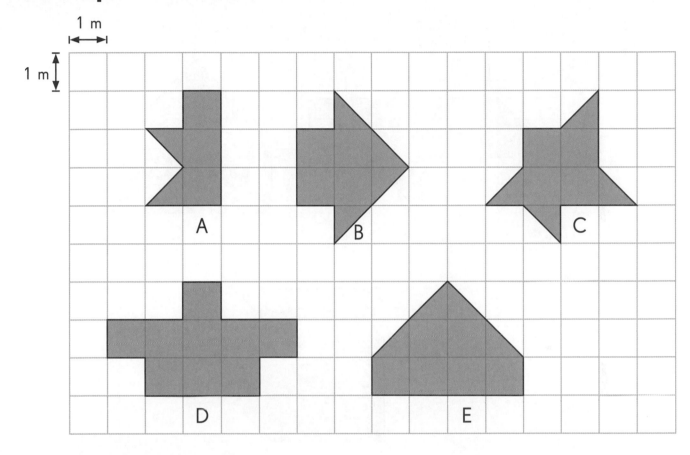

1.

Figure	A	B	C	D	E
Area	_____ m²	_____ m²	_____ m²	_____ m²	_____ m²

2. Which figure has the smallest area? Figure _____

3. Which figure has the largest area? Figure _____

4. Which figures have the same area? Figures _____

**Find the area of each shaded figure in square feet.
Then complete the table.**

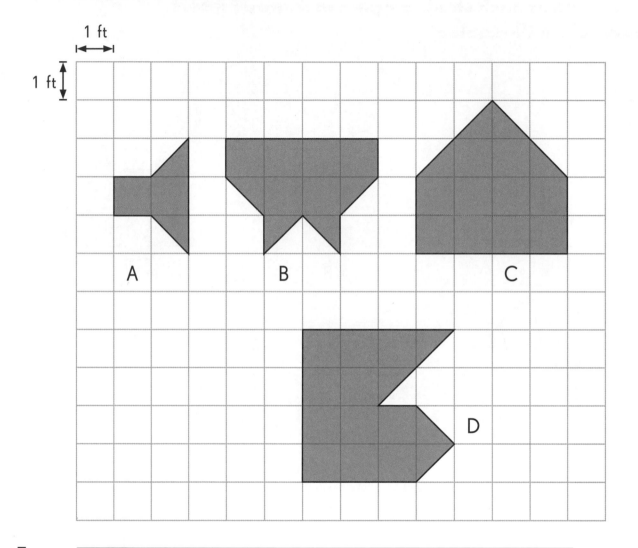

5.

Figure	A	B	C	D
Area	_____ ft²	_____ ft²	_____ ft²	_____ ft²

6. Which figure has the largest area? Figure _____

7. Which figure has the smallest area? Figure _____

Name: ______________________ Date: ______________

The figures are made of square and half-square tiles. Find the area of each shaded figure. Then complete the table.

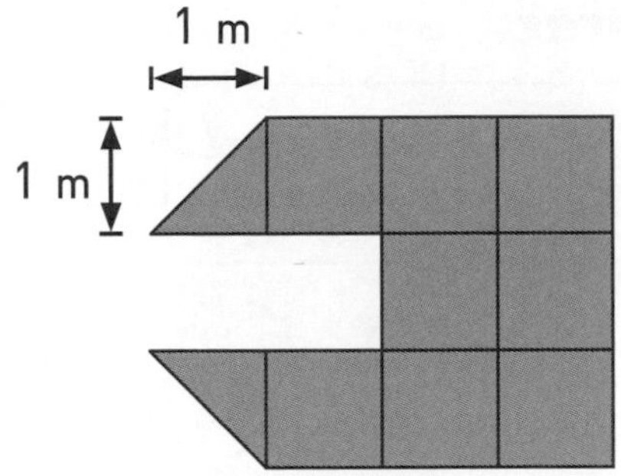

1 m
1 m

A

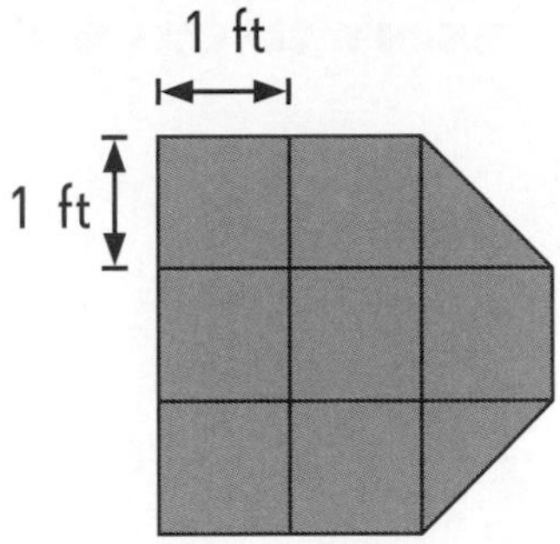

1 ft
1 ft

B

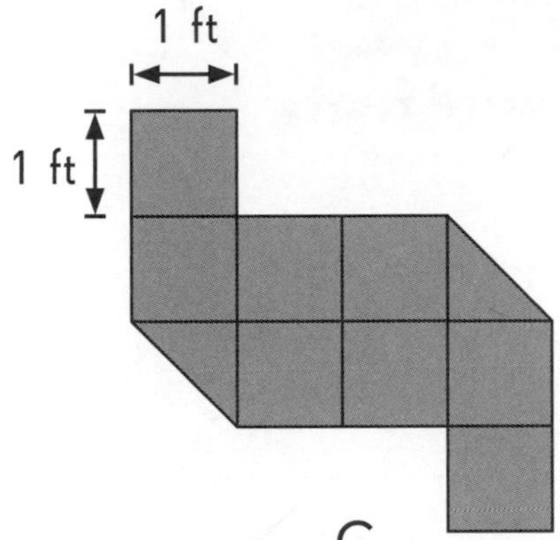

1 ft
1 ft

C

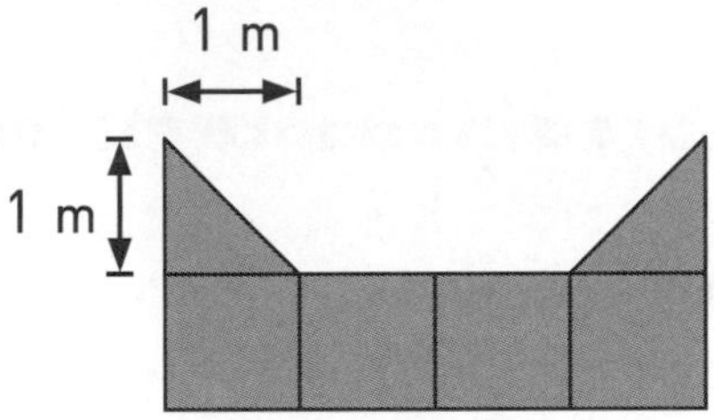

1 m
1 m

D

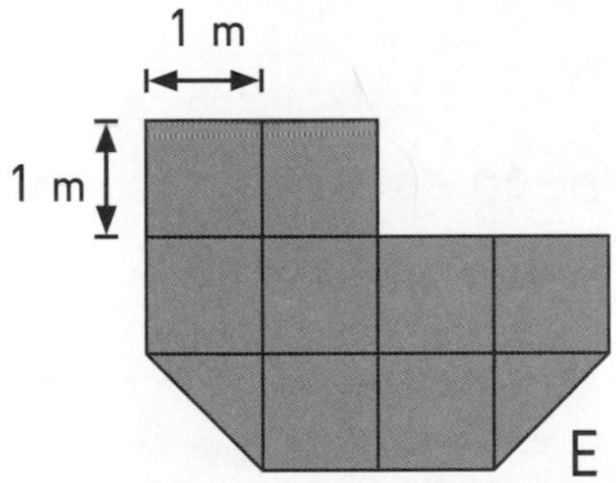

1 m
1 m

E

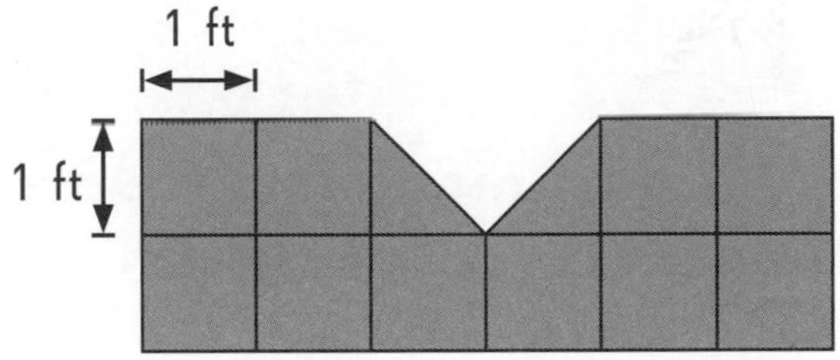

1 ft
1 ft

F

8.

Figure	Area
A	
B	
C	
D	
E	
F	

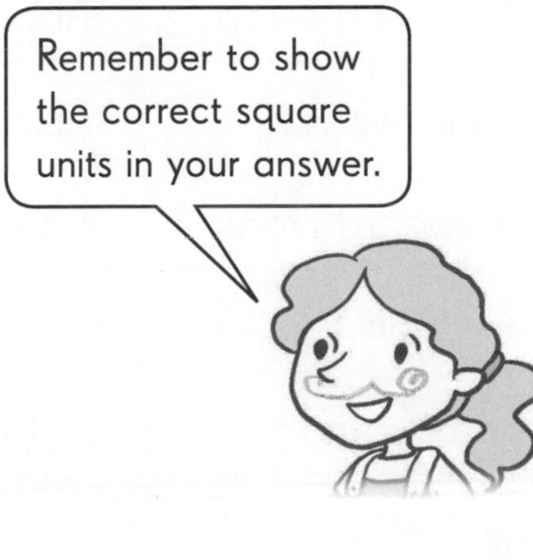

Remember to show the correct square units in your answer.

Make square pieces of paper with an area of 1 square meter and 1 square foot.
Use a ruler and scissors to cut out the squares.

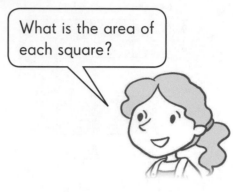

What is the area of each square?

Estimate the area in square meters and square feet.

9. Your kitchen floor

About _____ m^2

10. Your bed

About _____ ft^2

Use the square meter and square foot paper to estimate the area of these objects in your house.

11.

Object	Estimate	Check
Dining Table Top	About _____	About _____
Pillowcase	About _____	About _____
Cupboard Door	About _____	About _____
Television Screen	About _____	About _____
Bedroom Floor	About _____	About _____

Practice 4   Perimeter and Area

Complete. Find the perimeter and area of each shaded figure.

1.

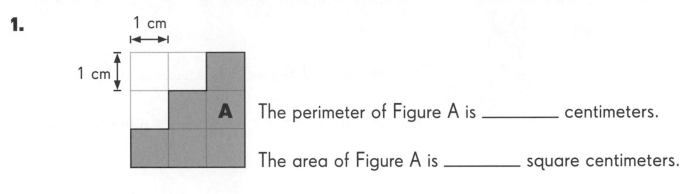

The perimeter of Figure A is _____ centimeters.

The area of Figure A is _____ square centimeters.

2.

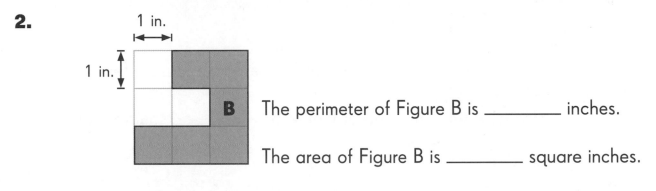

The perimeter of Figure B is _____ inches.

The area of Figure B is _____ square inches.

3.

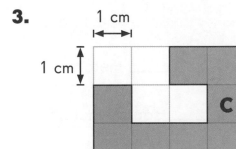

The perimeter of Figure C is _____ centimeters.

The area of Figure C is _____ square centimeters.

These inch squares are smaller than in real life.

4.

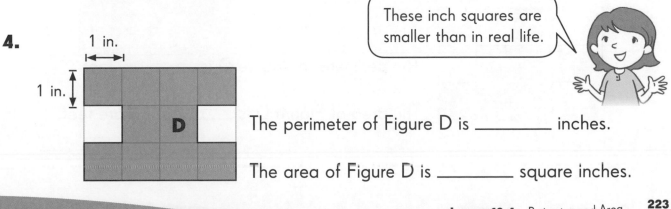

The perimeter of Figure D is _____ inches.

The area of Figure D is _____ square inches.

Complete. Find the perimeter and area of each shaded figure.

5.

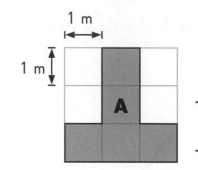

The perimeter of Figure A is _____ meters.

The area of Figure A is _____ square meters.

6.

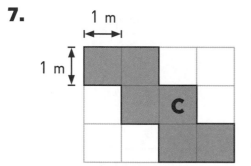

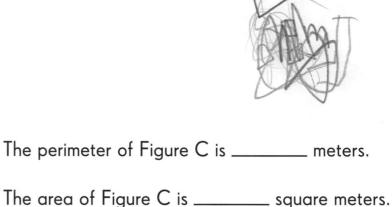

The perimeter of Figure B is _____ feet.

The area of Figure B is _____ square feet.

7.

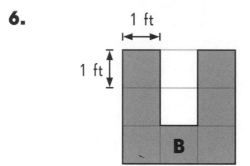

The perimeter of Figure C is _____ meters.

The area of Figure C is _____ square meters.

8.

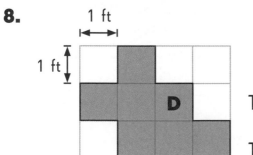

The perimeter of Figure D is _____ feet.

The area of Figure D is _____ square feet.

Draw two different figures with an area of 5 square centimeters.

9.

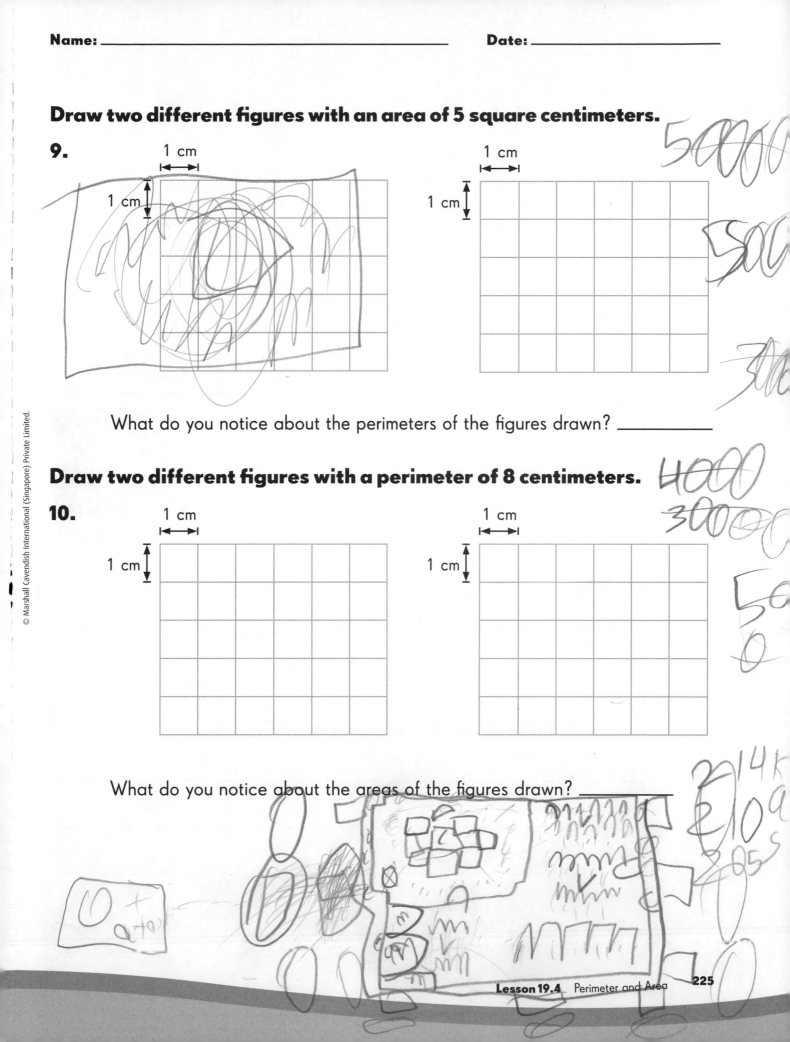

What do you notice about the perimeters of the figures drawn? _____

Draw two different figures with a perimeter of 8 centimeters.

10.

What do you notice about the areas of the figures drawn? _____

Find the perimeter and area of each figure.

11.

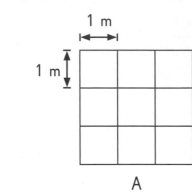

1 m
1 m
A

Perimeter = _____

Area = _____

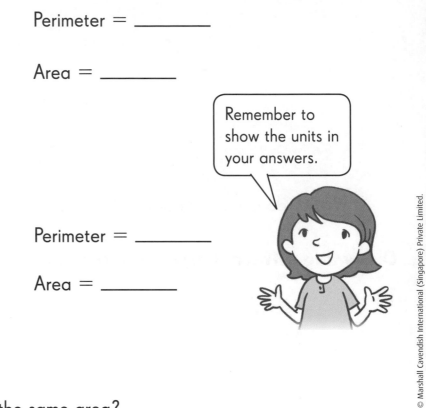

Remember to show the units in your answers.

12.

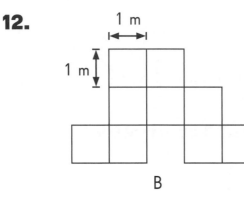

1 m
1 m
B

Perimeter = _____

Area = _____

Write *Yes* or *No*.

13. Do Figures A and B have the same area? _____

14. Do Figures A and B have the same perimeter? _____

What is different about perimeter and area? Explain.

15. _____

_____

_____

Find the area.

Example

Mr. Jones built the following koi pond in his front yard.
What is the total area of his koi pond?

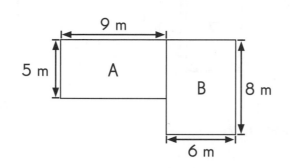

Area of Figure A = ___9___ ⊗ ___5___

= ___45___ m²

Area of Figure B = ___8___ ⊗ ___6___

= ___48___ m²

Total area of the koi pond = ___45___ + ___48___

= ___93___ m²

The total area of Mr. Jones' koi pond is

___93___ square meters.

1. Mr. and Mrs. Meyer want to build a pool in their front yard. They design the following pools.

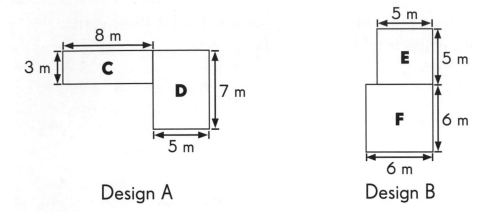

Design A   Design B

If Mr. and Mrs. Meyer want to build a pool with the largest area, which design should they pick?

Area of C = _____ $\bigcirc$ _____

   = _____ m²

Area of D = _____ $\bigcirc$ _____

   = _____ m²

Total area of Design A = _____ $\bigcirc$ _____

   = _____ m²

Area of E = _____ $\bigcirc$ _____

   = _____ m²

Area of F = _____ $\bigcirc$ _____

   = _____ m²

Total area of Design B = _____ $\bigcirc$ _____

   = _____ m²

Mr. and Mrs. Meyer should pick pool design _____ as it has the

larger area of _____ square meters.

Practice 5   More Perimeter

Measure the sides of each figure with a ruler. Then find the perimeter.

1.

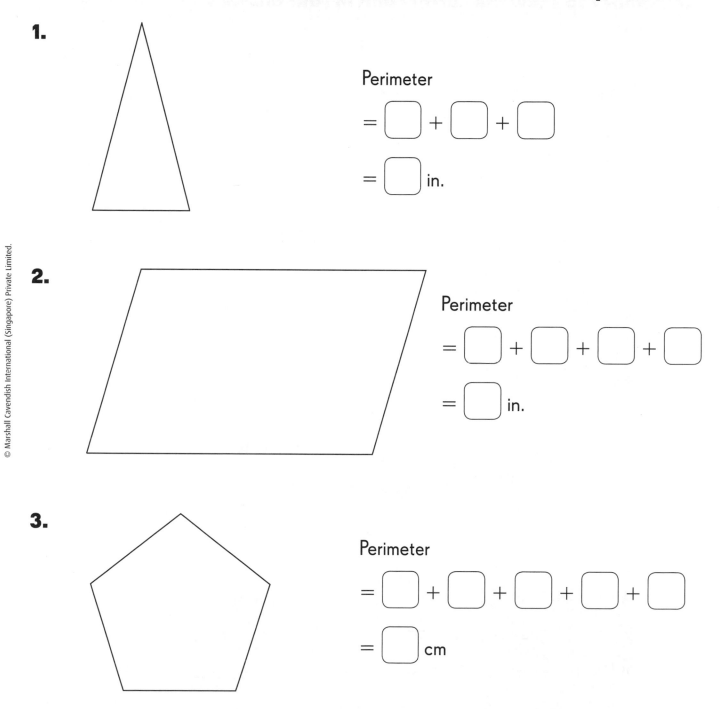

Perimeter

= ⬜ + ⬜ + ⬜

= ⬜ in.

2.

Perimeter

= ⬜ + ⬜ + ⬜ + ⬜

= ⬜ in.

3.

Perimeter

= ⬜ + ⬜ + ⬜ + ⬜ + ⬜

= ⬜ cm

Complete.
Find the perimeter of each figure.
Remember to show the correct unit in your answer.

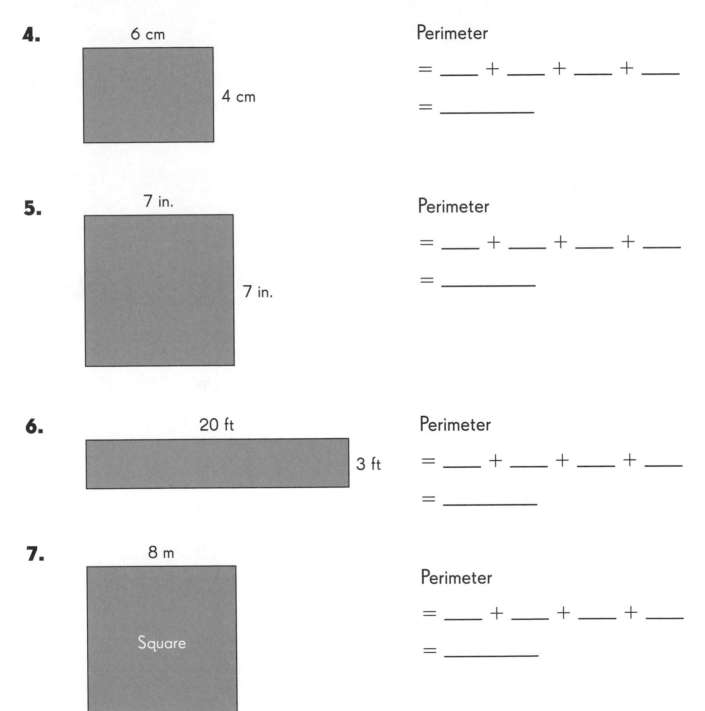

4.

6 cm

4 cm

Perimeter

= ___ + ___ + ___ + ___

= _____

5.

7 in.

7 in.

Perimeter

= ___ + ___ + ___ + ___

= _____

6.

20 ft

3 ft

Perimeter

= ___ + ___ + ___ + ___

= _____

7.

8 m

Square

Perimeter

= ___ + ___ + ___ + ___

= _____

Complete.
Find the perimeter of each figure.
Remember to show the correct unit in your answer.

8.   Perimeter

= _____ + _____ + _____

= _____

9.   Perimeter

= _____ + _____ + _____ + _____

= _____

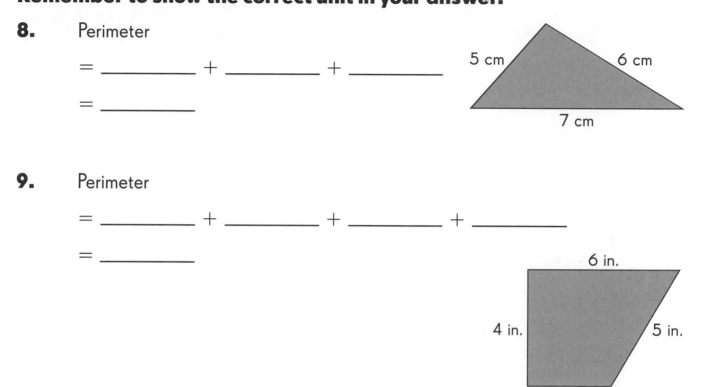

10.

11.

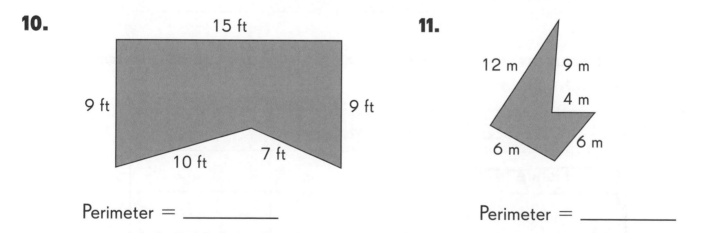

Perimeter = _____

Perimeter = _____

12. Use your ruler or a measuring tape to find the perimeter of each figure or object.

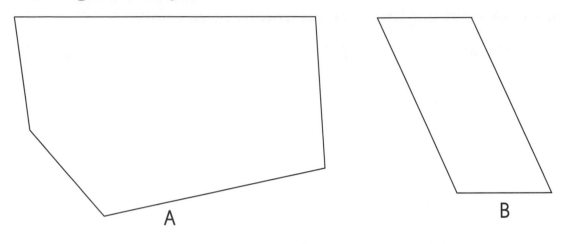

A

B

Object	Centimeter	Inch
Cover of your workbook		
Piece of paper		
Figure A		
Figure B		

13. Use your meterstick or yardstick to measure the perimeter of each object.

Object	Meter	Foot
Picture frame		
Bedroom door		
Table top		
Rug		

Solve.

14. Sean walks along the edge of a rectangular field once to look for his lost keychain. How far does he walk?

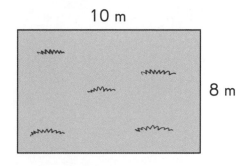

10 m

8 m

15. Alyssa wants to decorate this birthday card by pasting ribbon around it. What is the length of ribbon she needs?

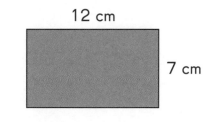

12 cm

7 cm

16. Owen has two square cardboard pieces.
Each side is 6 inches.
He places them side by side to make a rectangle. What is the perimeter of the rectangle?

Solve.

17. Theo wraps tape around the top of this rectangular box twice.
What is the length of sticky tape he uses?

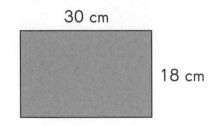

30 cm

18 cm

18. Each student in a group glued a string around a square with a
side of 12 centimeters. There are 5 students in the group.
What was the total length of string they used?

12 cm

19.   The length of a rectangular hall is 4 times its width.
If the perimeter of the hall is 20 meters, find the length and width
of the hall.

Length
Width

20.   Four square tables are arranged next to each other
to form one large rectangular table.
The perimeter of the large rectangular table is 20 meters.
What is the perimeter of each square table?

Math Journal

Look at John's answers for the perimeter of the squares and rectangles.

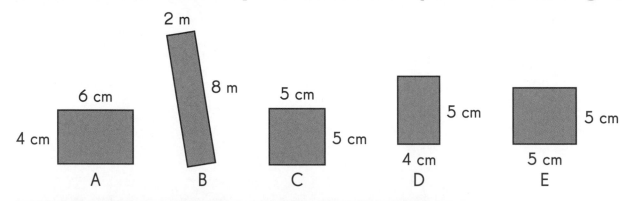

Figure	Length	Width	Perimeter
A	6 cm	4 cm	(10 cm)
B	8 m	2 m	(20 cm)
C	5 cm	5 cm	(20 cm²)
D	5 cm	4 cm	18 cm
E	(5 m)	(5 m)	(25 m)

John's mistakes are circled. Explain why his answers are not correct.

Write the correct answers.

Example   The unit for the perimeter of Figure B should be meter (m).

1.   Perimeter of Figure A:

_____

2.   Perimeter of Figure C:

_____

3.   Perimeter of Figure E:

_____

Put On Your Thinking Cap!

Challenging Practice

Complete.

1. Draw different rectangles with an area of 12 square centimeters.
Then draw different rectangles with an area of 9 square centimeters.
How many rectangles can you draw for each area?

1 cm

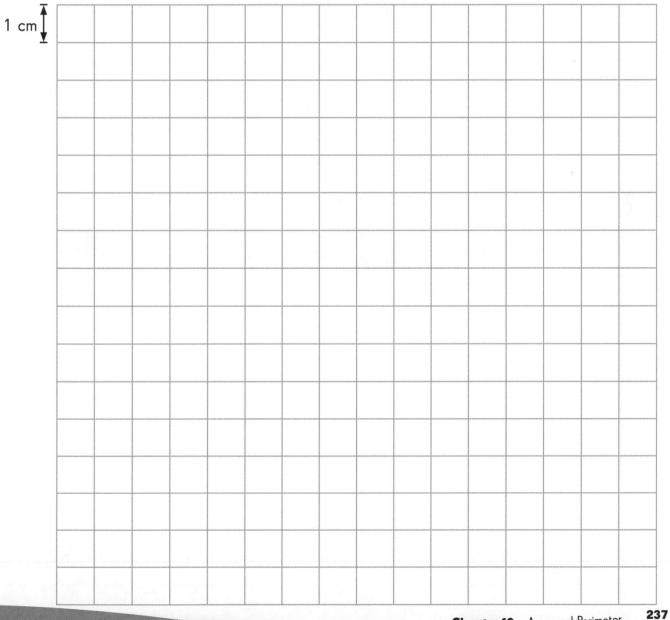

Solve.

2. Karl bends a piece of wire into a square as shown.

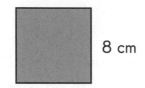

8 cm

Which of these rectangles can he make using the same piece of wire?

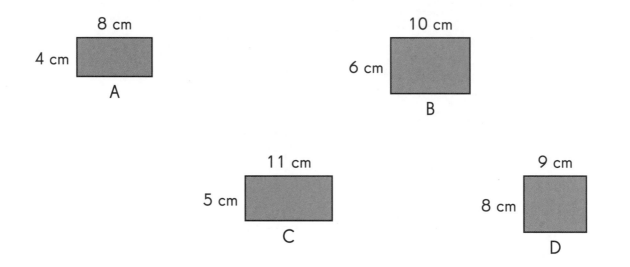

8 cm

4 cm

A

10 cm

6 cm

B

11 cm

5 cm

C

9 cm

8 cm

D

3.　　Ally wants to build an exercise pen for her pet rabbit. She has 36 feet of fencing to build a rectangular enclosure in her yard. She wants to carefully plan the length and width of the pen, measuring in units of whole feet.

Find all the possible ways that Ally could build her pen and have a perimeter of 36 feet. Fill in the table below.

Width (ft)	Length (ft)	Perimeter (ft)
1 ft	17 ft	36 ft

4.　　What are some of the concerns that Ally needs to think of in planning for the exercise pen?

_____

_____

_____

_____

_____

Put On Your Thinking Cap!

Problem Solving

Solve.
Look at this pattern.

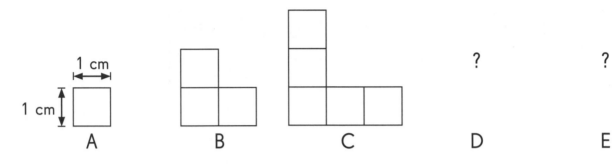

1 cm
1 cm
A   B   C   ?   ?
                                 D   E

What is the area of each figure?

Figure	Area
A	
B	
C	

If the pattern continues, what will the area of
Figure E be? Draw Figure E.

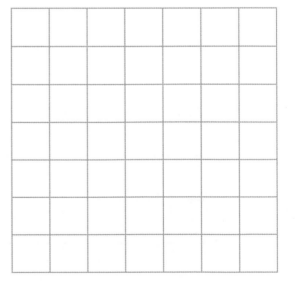

for Chapters 16 to 19

Concepts and Skills

Fill in the blanks with *past* or *to*. *(Lesson 16.1)*

1. 12 minutes _____ 8 is 8:12.

2. 10 minutes _____ 3 is 2:50.

Fill in the blanks. *(Lesson 16.2)*

3. 4 h 25 min = _____ min

4. 210 min = _____ h _____ min

Circle the correct number. *(Lesson 16.6)*

5. Jamie is playing basketball.

The temperature outside is about (32 , 72 , 120) °F.

6. Water freezes at (0 , 10 , 32) °F.

7. Gary puts on his jacket before he leaves the house.

The temperature outside is about (50 , 72 , 105) °F.

Complete.
Look at the angle. *(Lesson 17.1)*

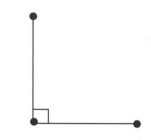

8.   Circle the angles below that are greater than the given angle.

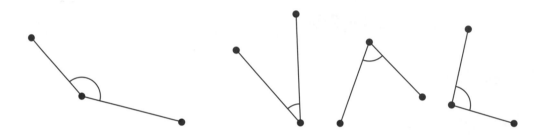

9.   Name the pairs of perpendicular and parallel line segments.

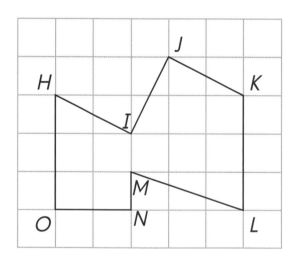

Perpendicular line segments: *(Lesson 17.4)*

_____

_____

Parallel line segments: *(Lesson 17.6)*

_____

_____

10. Mark the right angles in each figure. *(Lesson 17.3)*

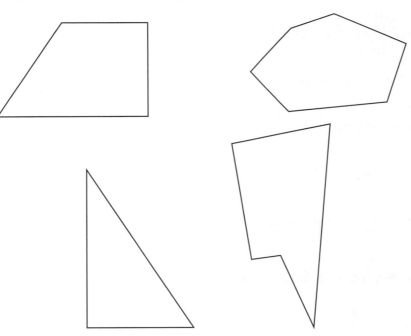

Circle the polygons. *(Lesson 18.1)*

11.

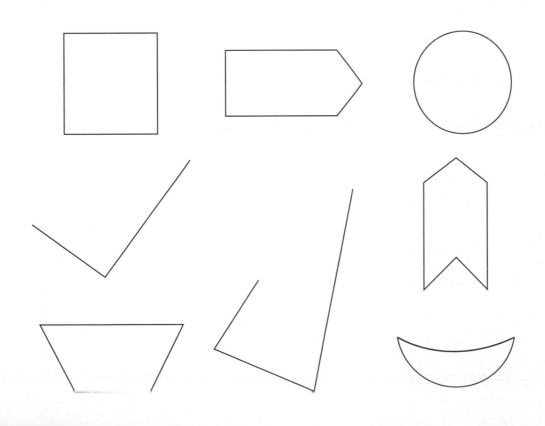

Write *true* or *false*. (Lesson 18.1)

12. A trapezoid has four angles.   _____

13. A circle is a quadrilateral.   _____

14. A rhombus has only one pair of parallel lines. _____

15. An octagon has eight sides.   _____

16. A square is <u>not</u> a rectangle.   _____

Does the figure show a flip? Write *yes* or *no*. (Lesson 18.2)

17.

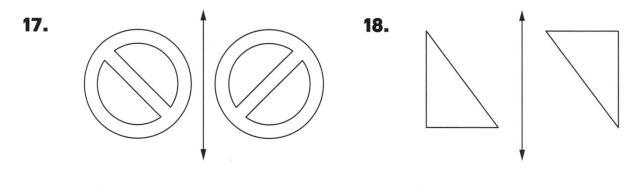

18.

_____   _____

Does the figure show a turn? Write *yes* or *no*. (Lesson 18.2)

19.

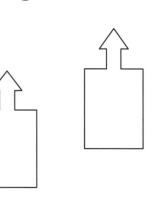

20.

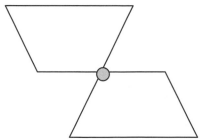

_____   _____

Circle the congruent shapes. *(Lesson 18.2)*

21.

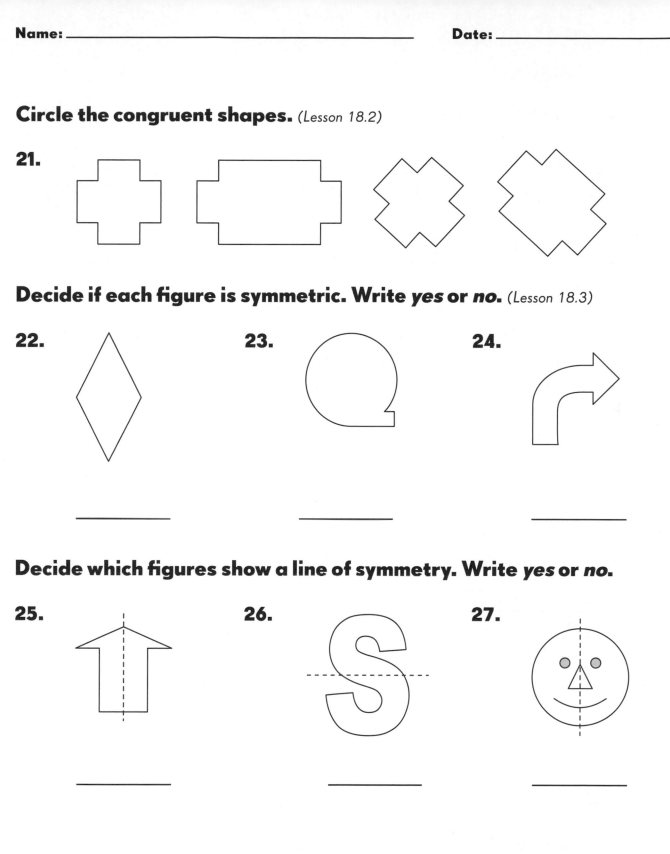

Decide if each figure is symmetric. Write *yes* or *no*. *(Lesson 18.3)*

22.

23.

24.

_____   _____   _____

Decide which figures show a line of symmetry. Write *yes* or *no*.

25.

26.

27.

_____   _____   _____

Find the area of each figure. *(Lesson 19.2)*

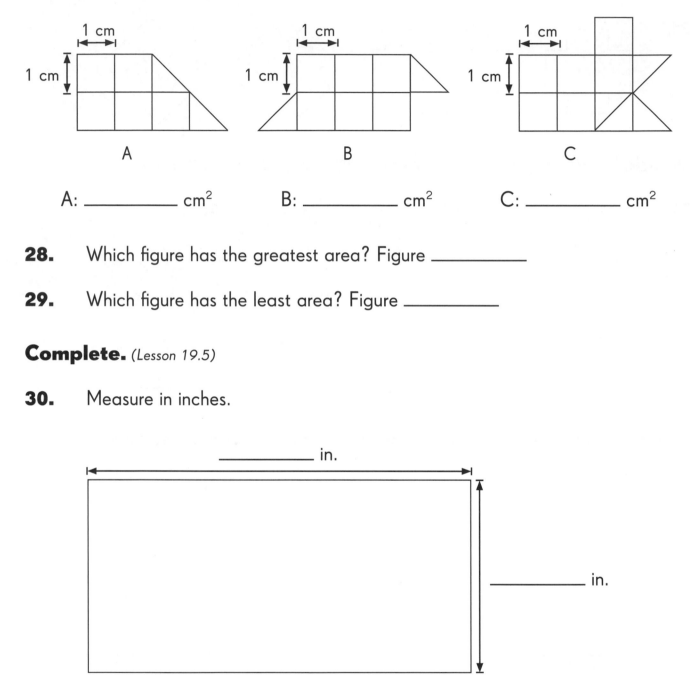

A: _____ cm²   B: _____ cm²   C: _____ cm²

28. Which figure has the greatest area? Figure _____

29. Which figure has the least area? Figure _____

Complete. *(Lesson 19.5)*

30. Measure in inches.

_____ in.

_____ in.

31. The perimeter of the rectangle is _____.

Problem Solving

Complete.
Draw two different rectangles with a perimeter of 10 feet each.

32.

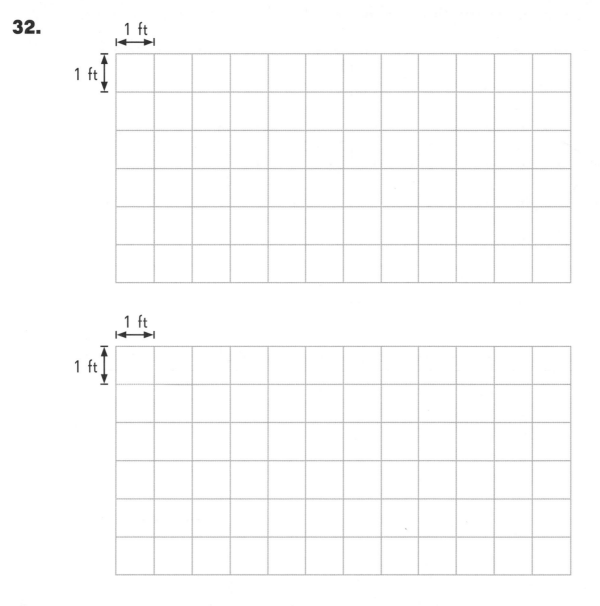

33.   Are the areas of the two rectangles the same? _____

34.   If their areas are the same, what is the area? _____

35.   If their areas are **not** the same, what is the difference in their areas?

_____

Complete.

36. Look at the shape in **a**.
How many sides and angles are there?

37. Draw another shape that has the same number of sides and angles.

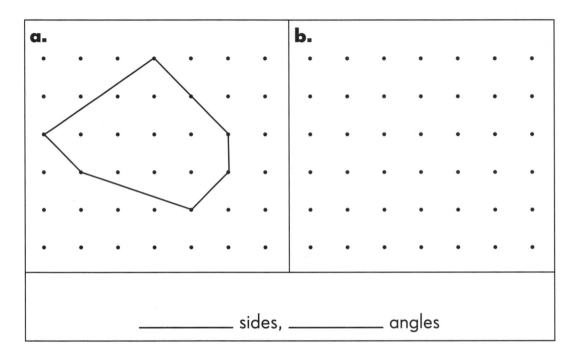

_____ sides, _____ angles

Solve. Show your work.

38. On Monday, Samantha spent 8 hours 10 minutes in school.
On Tuesday, she spent 6 hours 55 minutes in school.
How much longer did she spend in school on Monday than on Tuesday?

Solve. Show your work.

39. Laura sews six square patches to make a quilt, as shown below.
The side of each square patch is 15 inches long.
What is the perimeter of the quilt?

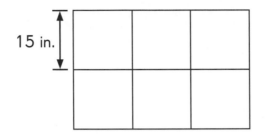

15 in.

Solve. Draw a time line to help you.

40.   Mr. Jones takes 2 hours 30 minutes to drive from San Diego
to Los Angeles. He reaches Los Angeles at 4:25 p.m.
What time did he leave San Diego?

Solve. Draw a time line to help you.

41.   Rhonda read a book from 8:45 A.M. to 10:50 A.M.

      a.   How long did she spend reading the book?

      b.   She continues reading for another 1 hour 25 minutes. What time will she stop reading?

End-of-Year Review

Test Prep

Multiple Choice

Fill in the circle next to the correct answer.

1. John spends $1.35 on bus fare and $2.50 on food each day. How much does he spend in two days? *(Lesson 10.1)*

   (A) $3.85   (B) $6.60

   (C) $6.70   (D) $7.70

2. Paige jogs around a 400-meter track 3 times a day. What is the distance she jogs each day? *(Lesson 11.2)*

   (A) 400 m   (B) 1 km 200 m

   (C) 1 km 400 m   (D) 10 km 200 m

3. Which mass is <u>not</u> the same as the others? *(Lesson 11.3)*

   (A) 7,220 g   (B) 7,022 g

   (C) 7,000 g + 22 g   (D) 7 kg 22 g

4. Which is <u>incorrect</u>? *(Lesson 14.3)*

   (A) $\frac{1}{2} = \frac{2}{4} = \frac{3}{6}$ (B) $\frac{1}{3} = \frac{2}{6} = \frac{3}{9}$

   (C) $\frac{2}{3} = \frac{4}{6} = \frac{6}{12}$ (D) $\frac{2}{2} = \frac{4}{4} = \frac{11}{11}$

5. Look at the measuring cups. *(Lesson 11.4)*

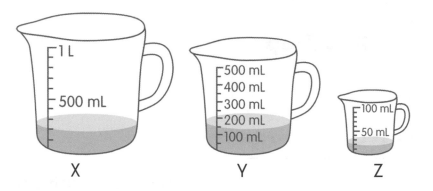

Which is correct?

(A) There is 500 milliliters more water in X than Y.

(B) There is a total of 1,500 milliliters of water in X and Y.

(C) Z contains 180 milliliters less water than X.

(D) The difference in the volume of water in Y and Z is 170 milliliters.

6. What fraction of the figure is shaded? *(Lesson 14.1)*

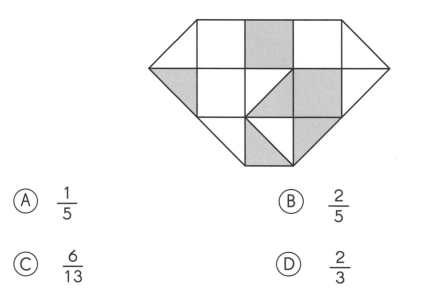

(A) $\dfrac{1}{5}$

(B) $\dfrac{2}{5}$

(C) $\dfrac{6}{13}$

(D) $\dfrac{2}{3}$

7.   Look at the line segments. *(Lesson 17.6)*

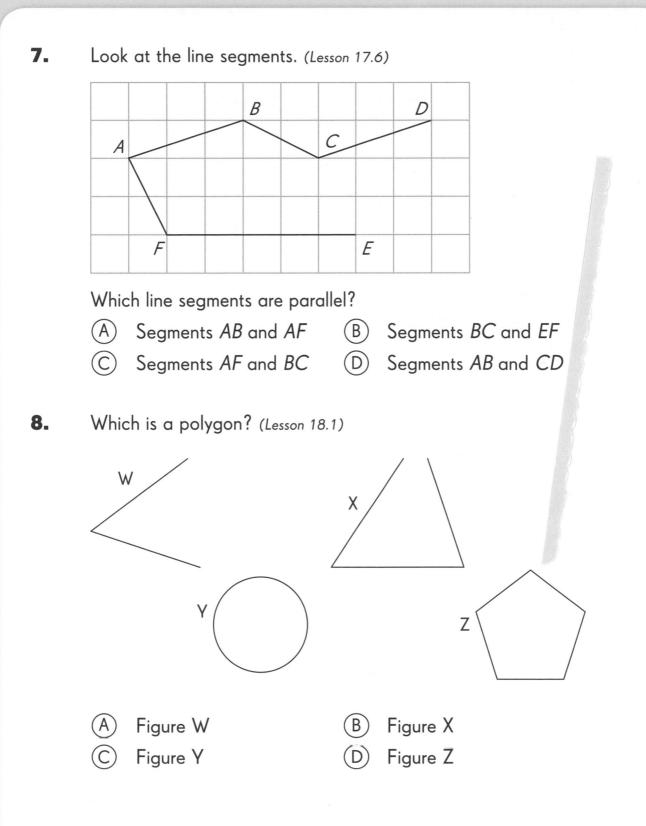

Which line segments are parallel?

Ⓐ   Segments *AB* and *AF*   Ⓑ   Segments *BC* and *EF*

Ⓒ   Segments *AF* and *BC*   Ⓓ   Segments *AB* and *CD*

8.   Which is a polygon? *(Lesson 18.1)*

W

X

Y

Z

Ⓐ   Figure W   Ⓑ   Figure X

Ⓒ   Figure Y   Ⓓ   Figure Z

9. Which tarts weigh the same? *(Lesson 15.2)*

Tarts	Weight
Lemon	2 pounds
Blueberry	3 pounds
Strawberry	24 ounces
Peach	32 ounces

(A) Lemon and Strawberry

(B) Lemon and Peach

(C) Blueberry and Strawberry

(D) Blueberry and Peach

10. 8 of the 20 buttons in a box are gray.
The rest are white.
What fraction of the buttons are white? *(Lesson 14.6)*

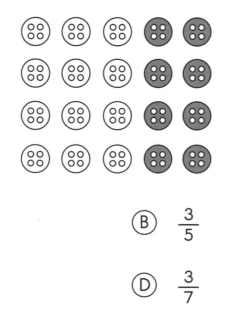

(A) $\frac{2}{5}$

(B) $\frac{3}{5}$

(C) $\frac{4}{5}$

(D) $\frac{3}{7}$

Short Answer

Read the questions carefully. Write your answers in the space provided.

11. Order the fractions from greatest to least. *(Lesson 14.4)*

$$\frac{1}{4}, \frac{7}{8}, \frac{3}{4}$$

_____

12. String A is 28 inches long. String B is 4 feet long. Which is longer? *(Lesson 15.1)*

String _____

13. George starts on his science project at 8:25 A.M. He finishes at 10:10 A.M. How long did he take? *(Lesson 16.5)*

_____ h _____ min

14. Mrs. Freeman puts 3 cups of lemon juice in a punch bowl. She adds 6 pints of water. How many cups of liquid are there in total? *(Lesson 15.3)*

_____ cups

15. Which angles in the figure are less than a right angle? *(Lesson 17.3)*

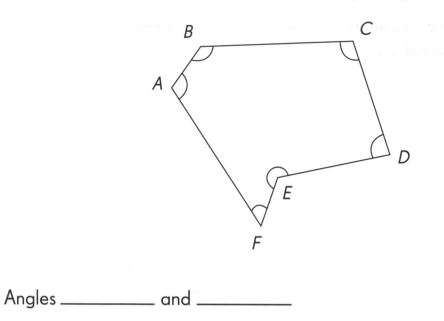

Angles _____ and _____

Look at the figures to answer Exercises 16 and 17. *(Lesson 19.4)*

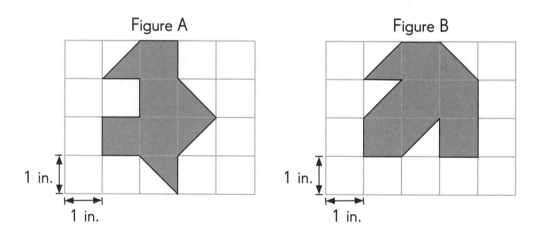

Figure A   Figure B

1 in.   1 in.

1 in.   1 in.

16. Which figure has a greater area?

Figure _____

17. How much greater?

_____ in.²

18. Which figures are congruent? *(Lesson 18.2)*

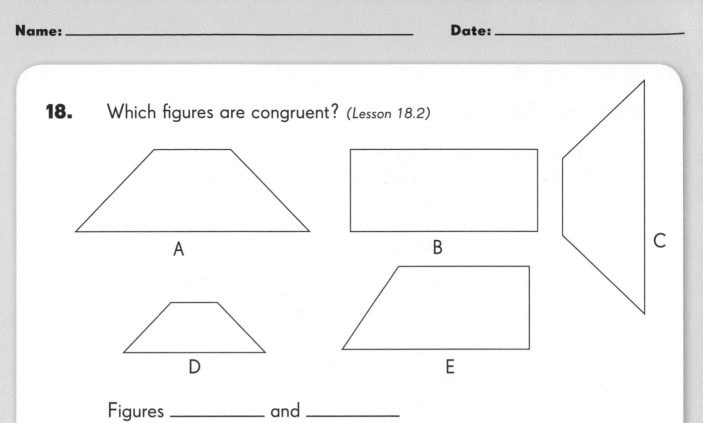

A

B

C

D

E

Figures _____ and _____

Look at the line plot to answer Exercises 19 and 20.

Beth surveyed her friends on the number of books they read last week. She drew a line plot to show her data. *(Lesson 13.3)*

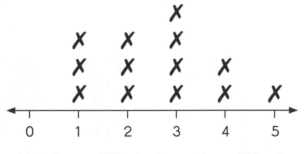

Number of Books Read Last Week

19. How many friends did she survey?

_____

20. How many friends read more than three books last week?

_____

Extended Response

The table and the bar graph show the number of books checked out of a library over five days. Some of the bars on the bar graph were incorrectly drawn.

Books Checked Out	
Monday	20
Tuesday	25
Wednesday	30
Thursday	35
Friday	40

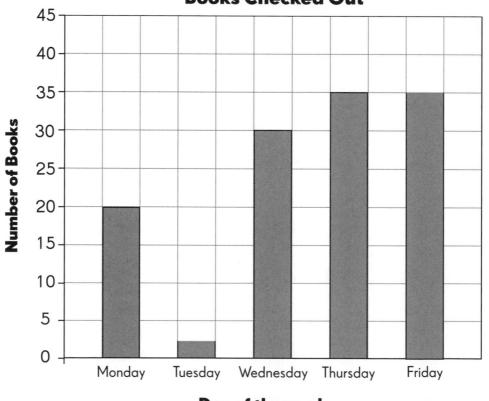

Books Checked Out

Look at the table and bar graph to answer Exercises 21 to 26.

21. Complete the bar graph for Tuesday.

22. One bar on the bar graph was incorrectly drawn for one of the days. On which day is it?

_____

23. Show the correct number of books checked out for that day in the bar graph.

24. How many books were checked out during that week?

_____ books

25. On which day was the number of books checked out twice as many as Monday?

_____

26. Look at the number of books checked out from Monday to Friday. What is the pattern?

_____

Solve . Show your work.

27. After a garage sale, Norman makes $105.50.
Julie makes $38.75 more than Norman. Lana makes $19.20
less than Julie. How much does Lana make?

28. Colin uses a wire to make a square. Each side is
6 centimeters long. He then uses the same wire to make
a triangle of three equal sides. How long is each side of
the triangle?

6 cm

Solve . Show your work.

29.   Pauline went to a party.
She spends 3 hours 25 minutes there.
She goes home at 2:15 P.M.
What time did she go to the party?

Draw a timeline to help you.

Solve . Show your work.

30. A family has two dogs, a husky and a terrier. The husky's mass is 23 kilograms. If he gains 7 kilograms, his mass will be five times that of the terrier. What is the mass of the terrier?